five things God uses to GROW your faith

PARTICIPANT'S GUIDE

Andy Stanley

ZONDERVAN®

NORTH POINT
RESOURCES

ZONDERVAN.com/
AUTHORTRACKER
follow your favorite authors

We want to hear from you. Please send your comments about this book to us in care of zreview@zondervan.com. Thank you.

ZONDERVAN

Five Things God Uses to Grow Your Faith Participant's Guide
Copyright © 2009 by North Point Ministries, Inc.

Requests for information should be addressed to:
Zondervan, *Grand Rapids, Michigan 49530*

ISBN 978-0-310-32423-2

Cover and interior design by Brian Manley (funwithrobots.com)

Printed in the United States of America

11 12 13 14 15 16 • 23 22 21 20 19 18 17 16 15 14 13 12 11 10 9 8 7 6

CONTENTS

INTRODUCTION
Touching Every Story

by Andy Stanley

Imagine for a moment that you had absolute, perfect faith and confidence in God—in a personal God who knew your name and always heard your prayers. Even when life was rocky and things weren't going your way, even when circumstances only got worse . . . imagine if the natural response in your mind and heart would be, *God's in control; he's going to work this out; he always leverages bad things for good purpose; and he has a perfect plan for my life. So I'll just wait patiently and see what he has in store for me.*

Think how different your life would be. Imagine your insecurities being replaced by increased confidence. Imagine the ability to remain calm when facing temptations and adversity, even tragedy. You'd wake up every day knowing God was absolutely bigger than all of that, always there to walk beside you through whatever you encountered. You'd have no fear for your family, your career, your relationships, your marriage, and your finances.

Wouldn't that be amazing?

A Little Irritating?

Maybe you've met people like that. They seem to have this mind-boggling, bulletproof, unshakable trust in God, even when they're going through horrible ordeals. There's something inescapably attractive about them, and we wish we had faith as strong as theirs. But we can also feel irritated. We'd like to try to rattle their childlike faith, to bring them back to the real world with the rest of us. We want to tap them on the shoulder: "Hey, there's more information you haven't thought about." It's just so hard to believe anyone could have such absolute confidence in God.

But that's exactly what God wants for all of us. He wants to explode our faith into something extraordinary. He wants us to have absolute confidence in him that influences every single facet of our lives.

And he's at work to make it happen.

Common Threads

So how's he doing it?

Over the years, some things have become clear to me and to those who work with me in ministry. As we've observed people and listened to literally hundreds of them describe their faith journeys, five things kept popping up in their stories. These five seem to be the things God uses repeatedly to grow people's faith.

We'll take a close look at all five in the weeks to come, but let me briefly introduce you to them.

First, there's the kind of *practical teaching* in which truth from the Bible comes alive with startling relevance to our everyday lives.

Then *providential relationships*—God puts people in our paths that shape us and influence us in extraordinary ways.

Third, when we exercise *private disciplines*, like prayer, personal time in the Bible, and even generosity, God uses them to deepen our relationship with him.

Fourth, God provides opportunities for *personal ministry* where we step outside our comfort zones to serve others—and end up receiving the biggest benefits ourselves.

And finally, *pivotal circumstances*—something big happens, usually something unplanned, unexpected, and unwanted, and suddenly our lives and the way we think about God are changed forever.

Now you won't find these five things tucked into some list somewhere in the Bible. And there may even be other significant elements besides these five that you would want to include. But in our experience and through observations over many years, these five in particular are ones that God uses consistently to take people's trust and confidence in him to new levels.

And since trust is the key to any healthy relationship, the result is that these people experience a new closeness with their Father in heaven. Their faith enters a different dimension—it becomes personal.

That's what God wants to do for all of us. So let's discover more about these *five things* he uses to expand our faith.

SESSION 1
BIG Faith

It's all about *trust*.

Right now, God isn't calling us to perfect behavior or to more knowledge about him, but to a *relationship* with him. And every healthy relationship is built on trust.

As we read the accounts of Jesus' life in the Bible, we see that he wasn't recognized and accepted by the most "religious" people—those who knew the Old Testament best, and who were recognized by others as being the best behaved. Their relationships with God were lacking in moment-by-moment dependence and trust.

Jesus pointed out their lack, and he found others who demonstrated in an astonishing way the kind of personal trust that God wants all of us to experience with him. This is about the simplicity of faith—and about God's commitment to expand this kind of confidence in him in our own hearts and lives.

DISCUSSION STARTER

Do you know people whose faith in God is so strong that you could sometimes describe it as *amazing*? What is it that makes their confidence in God so strong?

VIDEO OVERVIEW
For Session I of the DVD

God wants to take us to a new level of *big* faith—extraordinary trust and confidence in him.

The original break in humankind's relationship with God happened because of a refusal to trust him. God has been working with us on this trust issue ever since. His desire is to draw us into a relationship built around our absolute, perfect confidence in him.

In the Old Testament, God's reason for supporting the Israelites was so that they would show the world what it's like to have a trusting relationship with him. He established a trust relationship *before* giving them his laws and commandments.

Since that relationship broke down through a failure to trust, in the New Testament we see God working through Jesus to reconcile humankind back into a trust relationship with him. Jesus didn't tell us, "If you'll be good, God will love you and be your trustworthy God." Instead, Jesus was saying, "Trust *me* to reestablish your relationship with your heavenly Father."

Throughout the New Testament, God seeks to expand our faith. He's trying to teach us to trust him.

Greater trust makes all our human relationships stronger, and the same is true between God and us. It always comes down to trust.

Matthew 8:10 is one of the few occasions in the Gospels where we see Jesus *amazed* by something—and it's someone's *faith* that impresses him. The man who astonished him was a Roman centurion who indicated how well he understood the divine authority of Jesus. He asked Jesus to simply speak the word that would immediately heal a paralyzed servant back at the centurion's home. Jesus spoke the word, while also expressing his surprise at the centurion's extraordinary confidence in him.

> *When Jesus heard this, he was amazed and said to those following him, "Truly I tell you, I have not found anyone in Israel with such great faith." . . . Then Jesus said to the centurion, "Go! Let it be done just as you believed it would." And his servant was healed at that very hour.*
> *Matthew 8:10, 13*

God is honored and thrilled by our faith. So what is it that will grow our faith so he'll be increasingly honored?

Again, we believe there are five faith-building ingredients that God consistently uses in our lives:

- Practical teaching from the Bible

- Providential relationships

- Private disciplines

- Personal ministry

- Pivotal circumstances

It seems that God continues to make use of all five of these no matter where we are on the growth spectrum in our relationship with him.

So there's great value in placing ourselves in environments where these five are maximized. Being aware of them makes us more sensitive to what God is doing personally in our lives to expand our faith. And the greater our faith, the stronger our relationship with God and the deeper our intimacy with him.

VIDEO NOTES

DISCUSSION QUESTIONS

1. How would you describe the relationship between *obedience* and *trust*?

2. As you think back on your childhood, how was the *obedience/trust* relationship manifested in your home? Did you trust your parents? How did that impact your response to their authority?

3. Which is more important in a relationship: *trust* or *obedience*? Is the answer different depending on the type of relationship (marriage, parent-child, employer-employee, friends)?

4. Of the five things listed to make your faith grow, which has made the biggest difference in your own confidence in God? Why?

5. Has there ever been a time when your confidence in God—your faith—hit a really low point? Would you be willing to share that story with your group? If so, describe the events surrounding your loss of faith, as well as what helped you regain it.

6. What advice would you give a friend who has lost faith, or whose faith is very weak?

7. Think of someone you know whose faith seems strong. If that person later came to you and said he had lost his faith, what questions would you ask? If he asked your advice, what would you say?

MILEPOSTS

- Every healthy relationship is built on *trust,* including our relationship with God.

- God wants to take us to a new level of *big* faith—extraordinary trust and confidence in him.

- God uses five primary ways to expand our faith: (1) practical teaching from the Bible, (2) providential relationships, (3) private disciplines, (4) personal ministry, and (5) pivotal circumstances.

MOVING FORWARD

If you pay close attention while hearing the Bible taught or reading it for yourself, you'll often sense God saying the same thing: *"Trust me."* That's not to say the Bible's message is shallow and simplistic. Rather, in the various ways of responding appropriately and obediently to God, the most important thing he asks is that you trust him. Doing so may not seem to require a lot of faith when things are going well. But when life turns messy, is your faith leading you to depend on God? Or do you put your trust in something or someone else?

In the next several weeks, we'll discuss these five catalysts God uses to build that kind of faith.

For now, reflect on the most faith-building events and relationships in your own life. How have these affected your confidence in God?

CHANGING YOUR MIND

Can Jesus find this level of faith in you as well? God will put it there, if

you allow him to.

> *When Jesus heard this, he was amazed*
> *and said to those following him, "Truly I tell you,*
> *I have not found anyone in Israel with such great faith."*
>
> *Matthew 8:10*

PREPARATION FOR SESSION 2

To help you prepare for Session 2, use these suggested devotions during the week leading up to your small group meeting.

Day One

Glance through the "Sermon on the Mount" (the instruction Jesus gives in chapters 5, 6, and 7 of Matthew). What particular actions and deeds does Jesus call for in these chapters?

Day Two

In Matthew 7:24–27, look at the parable that ends the Sermon on the Mount. How would you express in your own words what Jesus teaches in verses 24 and 25?

Day Three

How would you express in your own words what Jesus teaches in Matthew 7:26–27?

Day Four

According to Matthew 7:28–29, how did those who were listening to Jesus respond to the Sermon on the Mount?

Day Five

Those who heard Jesus teach were never bored. In Luke 4:16–27, Jesus was teaching in his hometown synagogue in Nazareth. According to verses 28–29, what kind of response did he receive? Why do you think they responded that way?

Last Session

God takes us to a new level of big faith—extraordinary trust and confidence in him—through five influences: (1) practical teaching from the Bible, (2) providential relationships, (3) private disciplines, (4) personal ministry, and (5) pivotal circumstances.

Practical Teaching

When people talk about their spiritual journeys, a typical comment from them revolves around their initial exposure to someone who taught the Bible in a practical, life-impacting way. "For the first time," they'll frequently say, "I understood what the Bible means, and I understood what I was supposed to *do*." They began to actually apply Scripture to their lives—to their families, finances, work, morality, and ethics—and suddenly God came alive to them as never before.

They'll often say, "I believed this stuff all my life, but I didn't know how to apply it. Once I started doing it, I could begin to see God at work in my life."

What makes the difference in our lives is not simply gaining biblical knowledge, but being exposed to teaching that makes the Bible meaningful, practical, and applicable to everyday life—and then responding with action.

DISCUSSION STARTER

If you grew up attending church, was it a church that emphasized practical application of biblical truth to everyday life? Or was there more emphasis on something else like attendance, doctrine, or sacraments?

VIDEO OVERVIEW
For Session 2 of the DVD

When people tell their stories about God growing their faith, they usually mention being exposed to practical teaching from the Bible that triggered new and different responses. Suddenly, they see biblical truth as more than something to know; they realize, "Here's something God wants me to *do*."

In the New Testament, Jesus and the apostles taught for the purpose of application, not just knowledge. Jesus knew that simply knowing truth makes no difference; it's application that brings about change.

For example, in his Sermon on the Mount in Matthew 5–7, Jesus was saying, "If you really have faith in God, here's what you'll do and how you'll act." The entire sermon is strongly application-oriented.

It's reflected especially in the sermon's conclusion, where Jesus said that those who put his words into practice are like a wise man who built his house on a rock, which withstands floods and storms. If we want a difference in our lives—if we want our faith to show up in practical ways, if we want to see God at work—we have to *do* and not just *hear* whatever Jesus tells us. This contrasts with the common religious mind-set today that believes consistent attendance at church is what counts most.

Doing what Jesus says is a demonstration of *obedience*—which is really an act of faith in God. When our faith intersects with God's faithfulness, we put feet on our theology and begin acting on what the Bible says to do. God honors that obedience, because it's an act of faith—an expression of *trust*: "I'm going to do this simply because *you said to do it.*"

That's an expression of big faith. As a result, we see God's faithfulness in big ways. We see him at work in our minds and hearts and in visible, tangible ways throughout various aspects of our lives. But it doesn't happen until someone helps us understand how to apply and do what Scripture says.

That's why it's important to place ourselves in environments where we hear the Bible being taught, not just as something to know, but in the context of practical application: "Here's what to do, and here's how to do it." We don't need to learn theological intricacies; we need to be inspired to *do* something in response to what the Bible says.

What really affects our lives is not acquiring biblical knowledge, but obedience to biblical truth.

VIDEO NOTES

_____

_____

_____

_____

_____

_____

_____

_____

_____

_____

_____

_____

_____

_____

_____

_____

_____

_____

_____

_____

DISCUSSION QUESTIONS

1. When Bible truth is communicated effectively, do you expect it to be soothing or disturbing?

2. Read Matthew 7:24–28. This parable follows the Sermon on the Mount. Why do you think Jesus concluded his sermon with this parable? What does this strong exhortation say about Jesus' view of his own teaching?

3. As this parable portrays it, what's the relationship between putting Jesus' words into practice and having a rock-solid foundation? How would that be reflected in your life?

4. Have you ever applied a specific teaching of Scripture that, looking back, prepared you for an unexpected storm?

5. Can you think of a difficult time you've faced that could have been avoided if you'd applied the principles of Scripture?

6. How different do you think your financial situation would be today if for the past five years you'd consistently applied what the Scriptures teach about finances? And if you'd consistently applied scriptural teaching on relationships during that time, what would be different today in your marriage, family, or friendships?

MILEPOSTS

- The teachings of Jesus—and the entire Bible—are strongly application-oriented.

- For growing our faith, what we *do* is more significant than what we *know*. Obedience makes all the difference.

- Our faith grows when we listen to biblical teaching that is meaningful, practical, and applicable to everyday life—and then respond to it with action.

MOVING FORWARD

"Unapplied truth is like paint. It doesn't do anybody any good until it is applied." We can be the most learned of believers, but if our knowledge doesn't move us toward application, our faith will wither.

The Bible challenges us to respond to God's truth in many different ways, including loving our enemies, showing forgiveness, and practicing generosity. What have been the most difficult truths from the Bible for you to apply?

This week, identify two areas of your life where a bit more application would make a noticeable difference. And then apply.

CHANGING YOUR MIND

Commit to living each day like the "wise man" Jesus describes:

*Therefore everyone who hears these words of mine
and puts them into practice
is like a wise man who built his house on the rock.
The rain came down, the streams rose,
and the winds blew and beat against that house;
yet it did not fall, because it had its foundation on the rock.
But everyone who hears these words of mine
and does not put them into practice
is like a foolish man who built his house on sand.
The rain came down, the streams rose,
and the winds blew and beat against that house,
and it fell with a great crash.*

Matthew 7:24–27

PREPARATION FOR SESSION 3

To help you prepare for Session 3, use these suggested devotions during the week leading up to your small group meeting.

Day One

Read Proverbs 13:20. What does it mean to you to "walk with the wise"? And what does it mean to be "a companion of fools"? What is the stated outcome for each of these relationships?

Day Two

Look at 1 Corinthians 15:33. How have you seen the truth of this principle confirmed—in your own life, or in the life of someone you know?

Day Three

From what we see in Acts 2:42–44, what kind of relationship choices did the early Christians make?

Day Four

What kind of relationship choices are taught in Hebrews 10:24–25?

Day Five

According to Paul's words in Romans 1:11–12, what did he understand

about encouragement and faith?

Last Session

For growing our faith, what we *do* is more significant than what we *know*. So our faith thrives on practical teaching from the Bible that is meaningful and applicable to everyday life.

Providential Relationships

Looking back on your life, can you identify a particular person who helped spark your interest in God?

Can you think of someone God used unmistakably in your life to help make your faith bigger and stronger?

Most of us can identify people in our lives who were used by God to stimulate our faith in some way. Maybe someone helped you see that faith is bigger than you imagined. Maybe someone helped you recognize that God has a plan for your life that you needed to discover. Maybe you saw in someone's life an intersection of faith with everyday issues and decisions, and this amazed you and captured your attention. Or maybe someone was used in a powerful way to help you believe again after you'd lost your faith.

Looking back on such experiences, it's easy to see the importance of providential relationships at critical junctures in our lives.

DISCUSSION STARTER

What do you think are the most important factors that have allowed other people to have a strong influence in your life?

VIDEO OVERVIEW
For Session 3 of the DVD

Whenever we hear stories of people's faith journeys, we always hear about relationships. Discovering God is seldom something we do on our own, in total isolation from other people.

Of course, we always have a part. It's not like God forces his way into our lives through other people. But by his grace we can choose to participate and lean into those relationships, even though they can sometimes be uncomfortable.

God meshes our lives with the lives of certain other people, and the result is that our faith takes off as never before.

Sometimes these relationships involve only a single conversation. Other times, a series of conversations. Sometimes it's more about simply observing how others live. We see something unusual in their priorities and relationships and behavior, something very different from our own, and it moves us toward faith and God. However it happens, we can look back and see the providential way others' lives intersected our own. God uses human relationships to strengthen our faith in him.

The opposite is true as well; the principle works both ways. Certain relationships can undermine our faith in God, and we may look back with regret and see that they negatively influenced us.

Either for good or for bad, relationships are powerful. Unhealthy ones weaken our faith, and healthy ones build it up.

So what do we do with that principle?

We can ask ourselves, "How can I leverage my current relationships for the sake of building my faith?" As we do, we recognize that our culture tends to push us away from faith in God, not toward it. Our own nature mirrors the same thing; we're constantly drawn to wrong things instead of right things. So both our culture and our personal nature cause us to drift away from confidence and faith in God. That's why we need relationships that will influence us toward greater confidence.

The dynamics of this principle are reflected in Proverbs 13:20, which tells us that by walking with the wise we become wise, but companionship with fools will bring us harm. There's always a spiritual component to relationships; the people we choose to surround ourselves with always have the potential to impact us spiritually.

Since we have these choices, we need to be intentional about putting ourselves in relationships where God can work for our spiritual good. Such relationships may begin awkwardly, but looking back, we'll see that they were providential.

VIDEO NOTES

DISCUSSION QUESTIONS

1. Looking back, are there people you feel God providentially brought into your life at crucial times? Who are they, and how did God use them? Also, how have you seen God do this in the lives of your family members or your friends?

2. Can you recall a time when it seemed God brought someone across your path who could have helped you, but you resisted the relationship?

3. Are there people who would say God providentially dropped you into their lives?

4. In Proverbs 13:20, what's the promise to those who "walk with the wise"? And what is the consequence of "being a companion of fools"?

5. Notice that the first half of Proverbs 13:20 highlights what a person *becomes* ("wise") through associating with wise people, while the second half of the verse highlights what will *happen* ("suffer harm") through associating with fools. What is the significance of that distinction, based on your own life experiences? In other words, why doesn't that verse say, "He who walks with the wise becomes wise, but a companion of fools *becomes* a fool"?

6. I often tell our students, "Your friends will determine the direction and quality of your life." Was that true for you when you were in school? And how valid is that statement for you now?

MILEPOSTS

- There's always a spiritual component to relationships; the people we associate with always have the potential to affect us spiritually, for good or for bad.

- God has a way of bringing people into our lives whose influence can dramatically expand our faith.

- We need to learn how to leverage our current relationships for the sake of building our faith.

MOVING FORWARD

The promise from Proverbs 13:20 can be read alongside a similar warning from the New Testament: "Bad company corrupts good character" (1 Corinthians 15:33). The Bible makes it clear that certain relationships are pivotal in our spiritual development, while others can lead us in directions we never intended to go.

But we don't live in a vacuum; we're surrounded on all sides by wisdom and foolishness. Is it possible to completely ignore the companionship of fools? Our relationships with those who could be considered "foolish" might become pivotal in drawing those people closer to God. So how do you balance that with the recognition that those relationships also have the potential to inhibit your own spiritual growth?

What specific actions can you take this week to pursue the right balance in this?

CHANGING YOUR MIND

Who are the "wise" you need to associate with? Who are the "fools"

whose influence you should guard against?

> *Walk with the wise and become wise,*
> *for a companion of fools suffers harm.*
>
> Proverbs 13:20

PREPARATION FOR SESSION 4

To help you prepare for Session 4, use these suggested devotions during the week leading up to your small group meeting.

Day One

What practice or discipline does Jesus teach in Matthew 6:1–4? What guidelines does he give for it (explain this in your own words)? What outcome does he promise for doing it the right way?

Day Two

What practice or discipline does Jesus teach in Matthew 6:5–8? What guidelines does he give for it (explain this in your own words)? What outcome does he promise for doing it the right way?

Day Three

What practice or discipline does Jesus teach in Matthew 6:16–18? What guidelines does he give for it (explain this in your own words)? What outcome does he promise for doing it the right way?

Day Four

What more does Jesus teach us in Matthew 6:19–24 about our use of

money?

Day Five

In Mark 1:35, what kind of prayer discipline does Jesus model for us?

Last Session

We can trust God to bring people into our lives whose influence can help our faith grow strong, if we allow that to happen.

SESSION 4
Private Disciplines

Discipline—what a horrible word! And something we all love to avoid. It's all about what we're supposed to do but don't want to do.

When we meet people more disciplined than we are, on the one hand we're inspired; on the other, we're disheartened.

Yet things that begin as sheer disciplines in our lives can often become pleasing habits or hobbies (in sports or music, for example). Discipline brings progress and eventually results in freedom. Discipline means doing now what you don't like so that you can later do what you do like. Discipline is all about delayed gratification. And it has value even if we have a bad attitude about it.

When it's part of your lifestyle, what began as a discipline can later become a pleasure. That's especially true of certain private disciplines that stimulate your faith. It's a part of your spiritual journey that you can make a decision to be involved in at whatever level you choose.

DISCUSSION STARTER

If you hear that someone has a lot of self-discipline, or "is disciplined," what images come to mind: positive or negative ones? Do you think of this person as someone you would enjoy knowing and being around?

VIDEO OVERVIEW
For Session 4 of the DVD

When people talk about their faith journeys, they often mention learning to pray and to have a personal devotional time—a regular time set aside in their day to be alone with God. They also mention learning to exercise financial generosity, which usually begins in a gut-wrenching way.

These are examples of private disciplines. Jesus says their significance is in how they benefit us, rather than how we serve others by doing them. These private disciplines play a huge role in building our faith.

We naturally resist these disciplines. Recognizing that and meeting it head-on is good, because faith is like a muscle; the more you exercise it—stretch it, exhaust it—the stronger it becomes.

In Matthew 6:1–18, Jesus talks about the disciplines of giving to the poor, praying, and fasting. He emphasizes the importance of doing these things privately—recognizing that our heavenly Father, "who sees what is done in secret" (6:4,6,18), will himself reward us. If we do these things only to be seen by others, then honor from people (instead of from God) is the only reward we'll get.

The real issue is *trust*—our faith in God. For example, if we really *believed* what Jesus says about money, we would gladly be generous in our giving.

Most human beings have perfect trust in God regarding what will happen to them after they die. We trust God because we have no other options. Our eternal destinies are entirely in his hands. But in using our money and our time, we have choices. Right now, what we trust most is our own ability to control our environments and circumstances through our wealth. We live as if money means everything. Jesus tells us to trust him instead of our wealth, and we learn to do that only by letting go of our trust in money.

In the discipline of prayer, the trust issue is our use of time, our most valuable asset. God wants us to devote a portion of this priceless asset to praying regularly. He rewards us with the assurance of his presence.

In the discipline of giving, the trust issue is our use of money, our most coveted asset. God wants us to relinquish our grip on our finances in order to free us from greed and selfishness.

God wants us to trust him with our time and with our wealth. When we do, he will reward our faith.

VIDEO NOTES

_____

_____

_____

_____

_____

_____

_____

_____

_____

_____

_____

_____

_____

_____

_____

_____

_____

_____

_____

_____

DISCUSSION QUESTIONS

1. When it comes to discipline, in what areas of life do you struggle most?

2. Growing up, were you encouraged to develop habits that could be described as private spiritual disciplines—such as prayer, devotions, giving, fasting, confession? Which of these have you carried into adulthood, and which did you not? Why did they or didn't they "stick"?

3. Were you raised in a home where generosity was practiced and talked about? Were you raised to give? Was the giving in your home triggered more by occasions of need and crisis, or did your family regularly and systematically provide financial support to a church or to others?

4. How easy is it for you to be generous when confronted with a specific need? Why?

5. How easy is it for you to commit to giving a certain percentage of your income to your church?

6. Jesus promises that those who give according to his instruction will be rewarded. Do you feel you've been rewarded for your generosity in the past? If so, how?

7. Why do you think Jesus instructs us (Matthew 6:5–6) to pray privately on a regular basis?

8. Jesus promises a reward to those who pray privately (Matthew 6:6). What do you think this reward includes?

MILEPOSTS

- Practicing discipline in our lives results in progress, freedom, and peace. This is also true in the spiritual realm.

- Although disciplines involve routine, while relationships are fluid, disciplines have strong potential for deepening our relationships. This is also true in our relationship with God.

- The private disciplines of prayer, spending time with God, and giving financially will help our faith grow strong.

MOVING FORWARD

The notion of discipline being essential to an authentic, heartfelt relationship may seem strange. After all, discipline is largely about routine, while a relationship is fluid. But every healthy relationship is held together partly by disciplined actions and routines.

All self-imposed boundaries are a form of discipline. Perhaps the easiest way to understand the importance of discipline in a relationship is to consider a relationship without boundaries. Imagine a marriage in which neither partner practices self-control; that marriage would eventually deteriorate.

Our relationship with God shares a similar dynamic. Abandoning such disciplines leaves God at the periphery of our lives. Regularly practicing them, however, draws us into a closer, more intimate, more dependent relationship with our heavenly Father.

What will you do this week to establish both giving and prayer as regular disciplines?

CHANGING YOUR MIND

Look how Jesus values the disciplines of giving and prayer:

So when you give to the needy,
do not announce it with trumpets,
as the hypocrites do in the synagogues and on the streets,
to be honored by others. Truly I tell you,
they have received their reward in full.
But when you give to the needy,
do not let your left hand know what your right hand is doing,
so that your giving may be in secret. Then your Father,
who sees what is done in secret, will reward you.

Matthew 6:2–4

Very early in the morning, while it was still dark,
Jesus got up, left the house and went off to a solitary place,
where he prayed.

Mark 1:35

PREPARATION FOR SESSION 5

To help you prepare for Session 5, use these suggested devotions during the week leading up to your small group meeting.

Day One

Look at a busy day of ministry for Jesus as described in Matthew 14:13–14. Verses 15–21 go on to tell us what happened later that day. What do you think Jesus was trying to accomplish in the hearts and lives of his disciples?

Day Two

Look again at the incidents of one evening described in Matthew 14:15–21. How would you summarize the actions taken by the disciples?

Day Three

Look at what happened later that evening, as described in Matthew 14:22–32. Through what Jesus did and what he said, what do you think he was trying to accomplish in the hearts and lives of his disciples?

Day Four

In Matthew 14:28–31, look specifically at the actions and choices of Peter. How would you summarize these?

Day Five

What would you say are the overall lessons of faith that we can learn from what happened on the day and night described in Matthew 14:13–31?

Last Session

God uses personal disciplines in our lives—especially prayer (spending time with God) and giving financially—to help our faith grow strong.

Personal Ministry

At some point in your life, you've probably been faced with an opportunity to serve and to give your time and money to something bigger—something greater. Most likely, it was an opportunity to be involved in some area of ministry or service that was new to you, and you couldn't get it off your mind. You felt this inner voice saying, "Go for it," even though you felt unprepared and inadequate.

With fear and trembling, you stepped out and got involved. And you began to see your gifts and passion in service for a greater good.

Even now, you may be in a tug-of-war with God over something like that. He's inviting you outside what's comfortable, outside your skill set, outside your experience, in order to serve others. Yet the real issue is not about whether others need your service. The tension you feel is a faith tension. It's a trust issue. This opportunity for service is something God wants to use to stretch your faith muscles—to build up your trust in him.

DISCUSSION STARTER

Can you think of a situation when you were given a responsibility for which you felt inadequate and unprepared? How did it turn out? What did you learn about yourself?

VIDEO OVERVIEW
For Session 5 of the DVD

One of the Bible's most familiar stories is a strong example of how God builds our faith through personal ministry opportunities—those times when we're aware of a certain need others have, and we can't escape the sense that God's telling us, "I want *you* involved in meeting that need."

Beginning in Matthew 14:13, we read of a time when Jesus asked his disciples to feed a vast crowd he'd been ministering to. They pointed out their lack of resources—"only five loaves of bread and two fish"—but Jesus responded, "Bring them here to me" (14:17–18).

He says the same to us: "Just bring me what you have." We're discouraged about our inadequate education or experience or training or resources—but whatever we have, however small it seems, Jesus wants us simply to bring it to him, and he'll use it to meet the need.

After Jesus thanked his Father for those five loaves and two fish, he gave them to his disciples, who then distributed them to the people. His disciples simply did what they knew how to do, trusting Jesus to do something unusual—something only he could do.

When God brings these surprising ministry opportunities to us, our responsibility is simple: we're to do what we know how to do, then trust our heavenly Father to do what only he can do—believing that he can and will.

The tension we feel in those situations is simply our faith muscles being stretched. God is preparing us on the inside. He's working on our faith, because he cares so much about that. He knows that what's at stake is the size and strength of our faith.

This is the story behind every major move of God in human history. It's how he works. Afterward, we can only say, "Look what God did!" We give him credit for doing what only he could do.

Later in Matthew 14, we see this faith lesson deepened for the disciples when Jesus walks on the sea to meet them in their wind-tossed boat. Peter asked Jesus to invite him to walk out onto the water (14:28). That's the kind of prayer we can pray: "Lord, invite me out of my comfort zone." If we take him up on his invitation, we'll experience God in a new way; if not, we'll never know what he might have done through us.

VIDEO NOTES

_____

_____

_____

_____

_____

_____

_____

_____

_____

_____

_____

_____

_____

_____

_____

_____

_____

_____

_____

_____

_____

DISCUSSION QUESTIONS

1. Have you ever been asked to serve in a church or ministry-related context? If so, what was your initial response to that request?

2. Have you ever sensed God urging you to do something, yet you failed to do it? Why did you hold back?

3. Think about a time when you said yes to something God was urging you to do, although you felt unprepared for it. What was the impact of that experience on your faith?

4. Read Matthew 14:13–17. The disciples used their lack of resources as an excuse to question what Jesus asked them to do. What excuses have you used?

5. As you consider the disciples' initial response, what were they forgetting to factor into the equation?

6. Read Matthew 14:17–21. We see Jesus taking what little the disciples had available and going on to use it in a miraculous way. What talent, skill, experience, expertise, or ability do you have that, like the loaves and fish, don't appear to be things God could use in a significant way?

7. Who has chosen to serve you and invest in you in spite of the fact that he or she was busy, unprepared, or unsure of how things would turn out?

MILEPOSTS

- God builds our faith through challenging opportunities for personal ministry—allowing us to serve others even though we may feel unprepared and inadequate.

- The key in personal ministry is simply to do what we know how to do, and trust God to do what only he can do.

MOVING FORWARD

Personal ministry enables us to experience God's power in our weaknesses. We may feel unprepared, but these opportunities are incredibly rich experiences through which God grows our faith.

At first, you may perform an act of personal ministry or service in order to benefit others. But if you're like most people, you'll soon come to feel that you're the one who benefits most.

What opportunities do you sense God opening for you to become actively involved in personal ministry?

CHANGING YOUR MIND

Be encouraged by what God can do with what little you have to offer him:

And he directed the people to sit down on the grass.
Taking the five loaves and the two fish and looking up to heaven,
he gave thanks and broke the loaves.
Then he gave them to the disciples,
and the disciples gave them to the people.
They all ate and were satisfied, and the disciples picked up
twelve basketfuls of broken pieces that were left over.
The number of those who ate was about five thousand men,
besides women and children.

Matthew 14:19–21

PREPARATION FOR SESSION 6

To help you prepare for Session 6, use these suggested devotions during the week leading up to your small group meeting.

Day One

John 11 describes one of the most dramatic incidents in the life of Jesus. Read verses 1–6. What is most surprising to you about the words and actions of Jesus?

Day Two

Read John 11:7–16. How would you summarize what Jesus is trying to teach his disciples?

Day Three

In John 11:17–27, how is the faith of Martha being tested and stretched by Jesus? How does this compare with what you think he wants to do with your own faith?

Day Four

In John 11:28–37, how do you see the true compassion of Jesus?

Day Five

In John 11:38–45, what are the most significant things that Jesus accomplishes?

Last Session

God builds our faith when we minister to others even though we feel inadequate and unprepared. We are challenged to simply do what we know how to do, and trust God to do what only he can do.

Pivotal Circumstances

It happens again and again: people go through the most difficult circumstances imaginable, and come out on the other side with rock-solid, unshakable faith.

As they describe their stories later, they say, "I wouldn't have signed up for it; I wouldn't choose to go through it again; and I wouldn't wish it on anybody else. But God did something in the middle of those circumstances that I don't think he could have done any other way."

Hearing that, some skeptics might say it's just Christians trying to help God out. He's supposed to be a good and loving God, but bad things happen to his people, and there's really no valid explanation for it. He's backed himself into a corner.

But the fact is undeniable: our faith is permanently impacted by these big, bad, bold, unexpected circumstances. And that's not accidental; it's *intentional* on God's part.

DISCUSSION STARTER

Give a brief example from your life of an event or set of circumstances—positive or negative—that led to feelings of helplessness or being out of control. What role did God play in your thoughts? Did you pray? Did you pray differently? Were you angry? Was your confidence in God strengthened or weakened?

VIDEO OVERVIEW
For Session 6 of the DVD

The pivotal circumstances God uses to impact our faith can be either positive or negative. But most often, it's negative circumstances that cause us to turn back to God. Something begins to happen in a person's faith that maybe couldn't happen in any other way.

James tells us that trials are for the purpose of testing our faith, and that testing produces perseverance (James 1:2–4). We'd never sign up for difficult circumstances, yet they're the primary things God uses to strengthen our faith—if we allow him to do so.

The account of the death of Jesus' friend Lazarus (John 11) is one of the best examples of this in the Bible. Jesus actually creates negative circumstances in order to grow someone's faith.

After receiving word of his beloved friend's illness, Jesus unexpectedly delays going to see him. Instead, he allows Lazarus to die, and then tells his disciples, "For your sake I am glad I was not there, so that you may *believe*" (11:15). He was saying, "I'm willing for someone I love to die, and for others I love to have their hearts broken—*that's how important this lesson of faith is* that I'm about to teach you." Such a severe approach goes against what we want to believe about God.

By the time Jesus finally reached their village, Lazarus had been dead four days, and mourners surrounded his two sisters. As Jesus talked with Martha, she confessed to him her belief that God would hear his prayers. When Jesus told her, "I am the resurrection and the life" (11:25), he was telling her that he was the embodiment of resurrection and life. This was all about: *Who is Jesus?* "Do you *believe* this?" he asked Martha (11:26). It was a faith issue. *Did she trust him?*

The drama deepened as Jesus later talked with her sister, Mary, and saw her weeping and other mourners weeping as well. Jesus also wept (11:35). Instead of rushing in to do a miracle, he let them know that he shared in their sorrow, that he understood how they felt—just as he understands how we feel in our darkest trials.

Moments later, when he raised Lazarus back to life, Jesus confirmed for all time—and for all our most difficult circumstances—that he is indeed the resurrection and the life. He wants us to understand the incomparable importance of our faith, and he uses the tragedies in our lives to bring the lesson home.

VIDEO NOTES

_____

_____

_____

_____

_____

_____

_____

_____

_____

_____

_____

_____

_____

_____

_____

_____

_____

_____

DISCUSSION QUESTIONS

1. In *The Problem of Pain*, C. S. Lewis writes, "God whispers to us in our pleasures, speaks in our conscience, but shouts in our pains: it is His megaphone to rouse a deaf world." In your opinion, why is it so easy to factor God out of our lives when things are good and to question him when things aren't? Why does God almost always become part of the conversation when bad things happen?

2. Read James 1:2–4. James writes that trials test our *faith*—our confidence in God. What relationship do you see between adversity and a stronger faith?

3. James says that the goal of these tests is "perseverance." The implication is that trials can create *persevering faith* in God. But why trials? How else could God create persevering faith?

4. As you look at John 11:1–6, how does it make you feel to read that Jesus loved Lazarus, but didn't go to him in his time of need?

5. Look again at John 11:4. Is the idea of God using human pain for his glory disturbing to you? Is this a new concept for you?

6. As Jesus speaks with Martha (11:21–27), what do we learn that she already believes about Jesus? What more does Jesus want her to believe?

7. In John 11:41–42, what reason does Jesus give for pausing to pray before performing this miracle? What is the significance of that?

8. Respond to this statement: "When it feels like God is allowing something to happen *to* us, it is easy to lose faith. But when we accept that he is doing something *in* us, we are candidates for the grace we need in order to endure."

9. If God uses pivotal circumstances to build our faith in him, what should our response be the next time life takes us by surprise?

MILEPOSTS

•   God uses pivotal circumstances—both positive and negative—to impact our faith. Most often, negative situations have the most impact.

•   God uses the trials in our lives to test and expand our faith.

•   God is more interested in the growth of our faith than he is in our comfort.

MOVING FORWARD

Oftentimes, what shapes our response to pivotal circumstances is the support we have around us during these experiences. A community of providential relationships can help us see that God is not doing something *to* us, but something *in* us and *through* us.

Commit yourself afresh to a community of believers, growing together in faith.

CHANGING YOUR MIND

Hold on tightly to what's really true about your most difficult trials—because of God's love for you and his commitment to grow your faith:

*Consider it pure joy, my brothers and sisters,
whenever you face trials of many kinds,
because you know that the testing of your faith
produces perseverance. Let perseverance finish its work
so that you may be mature and complete,
not lacking anything.*

James 1:2–4

Leader's Guide

So, you're the leader...

Is that intimidating? Perhaps exciting? No doubt you have some mental pictures of what it will look like, what you will say, and how it will go. Before you get too far into the planning process, there are some things you should know about leading a small group discussion. We've compiled some proven techniques to help you.

BASICS ABOUT LEADING

1. Cultivate discussion — It's easy to think that the meeting lives or dies by your ideas. In reality, the ideas of everyone in the group are what make a small group meeting successful. The most valuable thing you can do is to get people to share their thoughts. That's how the relationships in your group will grow and thrive. Here's a rule: The impact of your study material will typically never exceed the impact of the relationships through which it was studied. The more meaningful the relationships, the more meaningful the study. In a sterile environment, even the best material is suppressed.

2. Point to the material — A good host or hostess gets the party going by offering delectable hors d'oeuvres and beverages. You too should be ready to serve up "delicacies" from the material. Sometimes you will simply read the discussion questions and invite everyone to respond. At other times, you may encourage others to share their ideas. Remember, some of the best treats are the ones your guests bring to the party. Go with the flow of the meeting, and be ready to pop out of the kitchen as needed.

3. Depart from the material — A talented ministry team has carefully designed this study for your small group. But that doesn't mean you should follow every part word for word. Knowing how and when to depart from the material is a valuable art. Nobody knows more about your people than you do. The narratives, questions, and exercises are here to provide a framework for discovery. However, every group is motivated differently. Sometimes the best way to start a small group discussion is simply to ask, "Does anyone have a personal insight or revelation you'd like to share from this week's material?" Then sit back and listen.

4. Stay on track — Conversation is like the currency of a small group discussion. The more interchange, the healthier the "economy." However, you need to keep your objectives in mind. If your goal is to have a meaningful experience with this material, then you should make sure the discussion is contributing to that end. It's easy to get off on a tangent. Be prepared to interject politely and refocus the group. You may need to say something like, "Excuse me, we're obviously all interested in this subject; however, I just want to make sure we cover all the material for this week."

5. Above all, pray — The best communicators are the ones that manage to get out of God's way enough to let him communicate *through* them. That's important to keep in mind. Books, sermons, and group discussions don't teach God's Word. God himself speaks into the hearts of men and women, and prayer is our vital channel to communicate directly with him. Cover your efforts in prayer. You don't just want God present at your meetings; you want him to direct them.

We hope you find these suggestions helpful. And we hope you enjoy leading this study. You will find additional guidelines and suggestions for each session in the Leader's Guide notes that follow.

Leader's Guide
Session Notes

SESSION I — BIG FAITH

Bottom Line

God wants to take us to a new level of *big* faith—extraordinary trust and confidence in him. He uses five primary ways to expand our faith: (1) practical teaching from the Bible, (2) providential relationships, (3) private disciplines, (4) personal ministry, and (5) pivotal circumstances.

Discussion Starter

Use the "Discussion Starter" printed in Session 1 of the Participant's Guide to "break the ice"—and to help everyone focus on faith.

Notes for Discussion Questions

Begin by having someone read aloud the story of the centurion with the sick servant in Matthew 8:5–10.

1. **How would you describe the relationship between *obedience* and *trust*?**

    Emphasize how much *trust* pervades everything God is after in his relationship with us.

2. **As you think back on your childhood, how was the *obedience/ trust* relationship manifested in your home? Did you trust your parents? How did that impact your response to their authority?**

    Allow plenty of time to recall and evaluate these earliest lessons about trust and obedience.

3. **Which is more important in a relationship: *trust* or *obedience*? Is the answer different depending on the type of relationship (marriage, parent-child, employer-employee, friends)?**

    The dynamics will vary in different types of relationships, but help everyone see that trust is a needed element in all of them.

4. **Of the five things listed to make your faith grow, which has made the biggest difference in your own confidence in God? Why?**

    Review and discuss these where helpful: (1) practical teaching from the Bible, (2) providential relationships, (3) private disciplines, (4) personal ministry, and (5) pivotal circumstances.

5. **Has there ever been a time when your confidence in God—your faith—hit a really low point? Would you be willing to share that story with your group? If so, describe the events surrounding your loss of faith, as well as what helped you regain it.**

Share your own honest response here, encouraging everyone to do the same.

6. **What advice would you give a friend who has lost faith, or whose faith is very weak?**

In both this question and the next, spend a generous amount of discussion time to uncover everyone's most significant values and principles regarding faith.

7. **Think of someone you know whose faith seems strong. If that person later came to you and said he had lost his faith, what questions would you ask? If he asked your advice, what would you say?**

You may want to conclude by focusing the group's attention again on the fact that God desires each of us to have a strong, growing faith.

Moving Forward

Encourage the group to evaluate their level of trust in God in whatever adversities or frustrations they face in the coming week.

Preparation for Session 2

Remember to point out the brief daily devotions that they can complete. They will help greatly in stimulating discussion in your next session. These devotions will enable everyone to dig into the Bible and start wrestling with the topics that will come up next time.

SESSION 2 — PRACTICAL TEACHING

Bottom Line

For growing our faith, what we *do* is more significant than what we *know*. Obedience makes the difference. Our faith thrives on Bible teaching that is meaningful, practical, and applicable to our everyday lives.

Discussion Starter

Use the "Discussion Starter" listed for Session 2 in the Participant's Guide. This question should help everyone in your group focus on the concept of applying the Bible to his or her life.

Notes for Discussion Questions

The premise of this series is that God uses five things to grow our faith. How many of the five can your group remember?

- *Practical teaching from the Bible*

- *Providential relationships*

- *Private disciplines*

- *Personal ministry*

- *Pivotal circumstances*

Then have everyone in your group answer and discuss the following:

1. **When Bible truth is communicated effectively, do you expect it to be soothing or disturbing?**

    Refer back to the DVD teaching on the fact that the teaching of Jesus was typically disruptive and disturbing.

2. **Read Matthew 7:24–28. This parable follows the Sermon on the Mount. Why do you think Jesus concluded his sermon with this parable? What does this strong exhortation say about Jesus' view of his own teaching?**

    Have someone read this passage aloud as you begin discussing the parable. Notice how his divine authority is alway assumed in what Jesus says.

3. **As this parable portrays it, what's the relationship between putting Jesus' words into practice and having a rock-solid foundation? How would that be reflected in your life?**

    Encourage the group to come up with various helpful images and descriptions.

4.   **Have you ever applied a specific teaching of Scripture that, looking back, prepared you for an unexpected storm?**

If you've seen this in your life, draw attention to what it says about God's care and love for us.

5.   **Can you think of a difficult time you've faced that could have been avoided if you'd applied the principles of Scripture?**

Again, your own honest answer here will help encourage others to share openly.

6.   **How different do you think your financial situation would be today if for the past five years you'd consistently applied what the Scriptures teach about finances? And if you'd consistently applied scriptural teaching on relationships during that time, what would be different today in your marriage, family, or friendships?**

Again, your own genuine response will be the best encouragement for thorough, honest answers from the group.

Moving Forward

Encourage the group to come back next week and report on new areas of specific application of the Bible in their lives.

Preparation for Session 3

Again, encourage your group members to complete the brief daily devotions. These will help stimulate discussion in your next session. They'll enable everyone to dig into the Bible and start wrestling with the topics coming up next time.

SESSION 3 — PROVIDENTIAL RELATIONSHIPS

Bottom Line

Relationships always impact our faith, for good or for bad. We can trust God to bring people into our lives whose influence can help our faith grow strong, if we allow that to happen.

Discussion Starter

Again, use the "Discussion Starter" listed for Session 3 in the Participant's Guide. This should help the group focus on the amazing impact that relationships have on our lives.

Notes for Discussion Questions

1. **Looking back, are there people you feel God providentially brought into your life at crucial times? Who are they, and how did God use them? Also, how have you seen God do this in the lives of your family members or your friends?**

   Allow plenty of time for everyone to answer.

2. **Can you recall a time when it seemed God brought someone across your path who could have helped you, but you resisted the relationship?**

    This may be harder to identify.

3. **Are there people who would say God providentially dropped you into their lives?**

    In a real sense, this is true for all of you in the group, in your relationships with each other.

4. **In Proverbs 13:20, what's the promise to those who "walk with the wise"? And what is the consequence of "being a companion of fools"?**

    Have two or three people read this passage from different translations. Biblically speaking, a fool is someone who knows the difference between right and wrong but doesn't care. A wise person is one who knows the difference and seeks to do what is right. Fools see life as disconnected; they live as if today's decisions have no impact on tomorrow. A wise person understands that life is connected; today's decisions create tomorrow's reality.

5. **Notice that the first half of Proverbs 13:20 highlights what a person *becomes* ("wise") through associating with wise people, while the second half of the verse highlights what will *happen* ("suffer harm") through associating with fools. What is the significance of that distinction, based on your own life experiences? In other words, why doesn't that verse say, "He who walks with the wise becomes wise, but a companion of fools *becomes* a fool"?**

    The "becoming" aspect can remind us that God's guidelines always result in shaping us into the kind of person he created us to be.

6. **I often tell our students, "Your friends will determine the direction and quality of your life." Was that true for you when you were in school? And how valid is that statement for you now?**

    As you close, ask each person in the group to pray a sentence prayer thanking God for a relationship he or she views as providential.

Moving Forward

Discuss the balance between not being "a companion of fools" while still being available for God to use in the lives of those who are distant from him.

Preparation for Session 4

Again, encourage your group members to complete the daily devotions. This will help them be better prepared for the topics coming up next time.

SESSION 4 — PRIVATE DISCIPLINES

Bottom Line

God uses private disciplines in our lives—in particular, prayer (spending time with God) and giving financially—to help our faith grow strong.

Discussion Starter

Again, use the "Discussion Starter" listed for Session 4 in the Participant's Guide. This should help everyone focus on the concept of private disciplines.

Notes for Discussion Questions

1. **When it comes to discipline, in what areas of life do you struggle most?**

   Take the lead in answering this one transparently. Disclose different areas of weakness as honestly as you can.

2. **Growing up, were you encouraged to develop habits that could be described as private spiritual disciplines—such as prayer, devotions, giving, fasting, confession? Which of these have you car-**

ried into adulthood, and which did you not? Why did they or didn't they "stick"?

Since strong human relationships are held together through discipline and self-control, we shouldn't be too surprised to discover that our relationship with God requires discipline as well.

3. **Were you raised in a home where generosity was practiced and talked about? Were you raised to give? Was the giving in your home triggered more by occasions of need and crisis, or did your family regularly and systematically provide financial support to a church or to others?**

    Our attitudes toward generosity, and toward money in general, are usually a reflection of the way we were raised. As you continue discussing this question, have someone read aloud Matthew 6:1–4, where Jesus challenges his audience to engage in the discipline of giving. Jesus assumes generosity. Notice he says "when" you give, not "if."

4. **How easy is it for you to be generous when confronted with a specific need? Why?**

    What's the value of this kind of giving?

5.   **How easy is it for you to commit to giving a certain percentage of your income to your church?**

Refer back to the challenge given in the DVD teaching for committing to give a percentage of your income for one month. What is your reaction to that challenge?

6.   **Jesus promises that those who give according to his instruction will be rewarded. Do you feel you've been rewarded for your generosity in the past? If so, how?**

This will likely bring in the topic of eternal rewards—those we'll never know about in this life.

7.   **Why do you think Jesus instructs us (Matthew 6:5–6) to pray privately on a regular basis?**

Have someone read Matthew 6:5–6 and Mark 1:35. Following his discussion on giving, Jesus challenges his audience to engage in the discipline of private prayer.

8.   **Jesus promises a reward to those who pray privately (Matthew 6:6). What do you think this reward includes?**

What is your group's reaction to the challenge (in the DVD

teaching) to be involved in daily prayer? Consider committing as a group to do this for one week.

Moving Forward

Encourage your group's deliberate, proactive commitment to giving and prayer. How can you hold each other accountable?

Preparation for Session 5

Again, encourage your group members to complete the daily devotions in preparation for the next session.

SESSION 5 — PERSONAL MINISTRY

Bottom Line

God builds our faith when we minister to others even though we feel inadequate and unprepared. We simply do what we know how to do, and trust God to do what only he can do.

Discussion Starter

Again, use the "Discussion Starter" listed for Session 5 in the Participant's Guide. This should help everyone focus on the concept of stepping outside our comfort and expertise to take on new opportunities.

Notes for Discussion Questions

Remind the group that a growing faith is the essence of a growing relationship with Christ—and that these are dynamics God uses to build our faith:

- *Practical teaching*

- *Providential relationships*

- *Private disciplines*

- *Personal ministry*

- *Pivotal circumstances*

1. **Have you ever been asked to serve in a church or ministry-related context? If so, what was your initial response to that request?**

   The goal is to surface the tension we feel when God is urging us to serve in a setting for which we feel unprepared or inadequate.

2. **Have you ever sensed God urging you to do something, yet you failed to do it? Why did you hold back?**

   Let your own honest answer lead the way for others.

3. **Think about a time when you said yes to something God was urging you to do, although you felt unprepared for it. What was the impact of that experience on your faith?**

   Allow plenty of time for everyone to answer this one fully. Help them recognize from their own experiences the value of personal ministry.

4. **Read Matthew 14:13–17. The disciples used their lack of resources as an excuse to question what Jesus asked them to do. What excuses have you used?**

   Read aloud this passage, where we find Jesus asking his disciples to do something that was actually impossible for them to do.

5. **As you consider the disciples' initial response, what were they forgetting to factor into the equation?**

    The disciples went on to give Jesus the little that they had to work with. Jesus blessed it, then gave it back to them to distribute to the people. No one standing there that day would have considered those few fish and loaves as things Jesus would use in a miraculous way. But he did.

6. **Read Matthew 14:17–21. We see Jesus taking what little the disciples had available and going on to use it in a miraculous way. What talent, skill, experience, expertise, or ability do you have that, like the loaves and fish, don't appear to be things God could use in a significant way?**

    Read the passage aloud and then discuss what this experience must have been like for the disciples.

7. **Who has chosen to serve you and invest in you in spite of the fact that he or she was busy, unprepared, or unsure of how things would turn out?**

    Encourage grateful recognition for those who have served your group members in this way. Spend time together in prayer to express your gratitude to God.

Moving Forward

Have group members pray a sentence prayer making their skills, talents, or experience available to God to use as he sees fit. Or have group members simply express their availability to God to be used in his service.

Preparation for Session 6

Once more, encourage your group members to complete the daily devotions in preparation for the next session.

SESSION 6 — PIVOTAL CIRCUMSTANCES

Bottom Line

God brings trials into our lives to test and expand our faith. He is more interested in the growth of our faith than he is in our comfort.

Discussion Starter

This should help the group begin to focus on God's involvement in the negative circumstances that can overwhelm our lives. Encourage group members not to sugarcoat their stories. Anger or bitterness and retreating from God are all natural responses.

Notes for Discussion Questions

1. In *The Problem of Pain*, C. S. Lewis writes, "God whispers to us in our pleasures, speaks in our conscience, but shouts in our pains: it is His megaphone to rouse a deaf world." In your opinion, why is it so easy to factor God out of our lives when things are good and to question him when things aren't? Why does God almost always become part of the conversation when bad things happen?

    Why is it necessary for God to "shout" at us by using our pain?

2.   **Read James 1:2–4. James writes that trials test our *faith*—our confidence in God. What relationship do you see between adversity and a stronger faith?**

Have someone read this passage aloud. Notice God's design and purpose for the trials he allows into our lives.

3.   **James says that the goal of these tests is "perseverance." The implication is that trials can create persevering *faith* in God. But why trials? How else could God create persevering faith?**

The answer you arrive at together may be "None." (Note the example of Jesus in Hebrews 5:8.)

4.   **As you look at John 11:1–6, how does it make you feel to read that Jesus loved Lazarus, but didn't go to him in his time of need?**

Have someone read this passage aloud, and continue doing the same with the passages that relate to the following questions.

5.   **Look again at John 11:4. Is the idea of God using human pain for his glory disturbing to you? Is this a new concept for you?**

This passage indicates how important God's glory is to him. How important is his glory to you?

6. **As Jesus speaks with Martha (11:21–27), what do we learn that she already believes about Jesus? What more does Jesus want her to believe?**

    Have someone read aloud verses 17–32 for the full interaction Jesus had with Martha and Mary.

7. **In John 11:41–42, what reason does Jesus give for pausing to pray before performing this miracle? What is the significance of that?**

    For the context here, have someone read all of verses 33–44.

8. **Respond to this statement: "When it feels like God is allowing something to happen *to* us, it is easy to lose faith. But when we accept that he is doing something *in* us, we are candidates for the grace we need in order to endure."**

    Encourage the group to recognize and identify the kinds of things God is doing in each person.

9. **If God uses pivotal circumstances to build our faith in him, what should our response be the next time life takes us by surprise?**

    As you close, allow plenty of time for a thorough review of this study and its degree of helpfulness for everyone in your group.

Moving Forward

Close your group time by praying for the individuals or couples in your

group who are currently facing faith-stretching trials.

apexart

Cautionary Tales:
Critical Curating

Cautionary Tales: Critical Curating
Edited by Steven Rand and Heather Kouris
ISBN: 1-933347-10-4
1. Curatorial Studies 2. Art History

Printed in U.S.A.

apexart

291 Church Street
New York, NY 10013
t: 212 431 5270
f: 696 827 2487
www.apexart.org
info@apexart.org

Contents

apexart is a 501(c)(3) nonprofit visual arts organization founded in 1994 by artist Steven Rand. Over the years it has evolved from a NYC exhibition venue to include an international residency program, public programs, and a conference program. This year we extend our programming to book publishing, having first produced *On Cultural Influence*, a collection of essays from past conferences. *Cautionary Tales: Critical Curating* is the second in this series that explore topics in the visual arts. Special thanks to David Levi Strauss for his advice on this publication and to NLW for continued support.

Steven Rand

Preface

I started apexart in 1994 so I could go to a place like apexart. The intent was to be idea-centric and invite artists, writers, and others to be in the role of a curator. The thought was that everyone had "one good show in them," much like the saying "everyone has one good book."

In a program shift during the late 90s, we began to invite the new group of independent international curators coming from programs such as de Appel in The Netherlands, Bard College in New York, and others, in addition to numerous individuals working and learning on their own. De Apple is a seven-month program while Bard is a two-year program that awards an M.A. degree. The intent was to show in New York City what was being seen in Europe and Asia, and to experience and assess it.

While this is now a ubiquitous practice, this was not the case at that time, and apexart is now returning to its earlier ideology and including content outside the contemporary art world. We will continue our "Unsolicited Proposal" program to serve the curatorial community, creating programming for two exhibitions each year. More about this can be viewed on our website.

I mentioned to a past director of a curatorial program that we are doing a curator book and the reaction was, "Just what we don't need." I agree and hope that you do not find this "just another curator book."

It started with the idea to ask ten individuals to write what they would like to say to someone considering a career in curatorial studies. Not how to curate, but what to consider, what to look out for, to avoid, or to reconsider. This seemed especially important being ten years into a profession with conclusions and observations being made about the value and efficacy of the practice. The authors take different paths, defining the practice, describing it, and being critical of it. They speak to the potential of what it can be and what it means to them. Some are more cautionary than others.

Most curatorial programs consist of considering social theory and philosophy and the dynamics of organizing an exhibition. Often the issues discussed and values considered are very pragmatic. Support of artists is more productive than criticism, creating opportunity is more satisfying than fulfilling opportunity, production becomes more important than creativity, and recognition more than personal satisfaction. Political affiliations within the field and an urgency of career have replaced time-consuming research in less popular, though more diverse and disparate topics. To some degree this is understandable in that it reflects the values and insecurities in society today, but it may not bode well for creativity in the arts. It seems that the study of history has been receding in high schools for years because of a sense that so much happens in such a short period that experience is preferable to overview and the consideration of history unnecessary.

Similarly, the interest in art history has been abating while there has been an increase in interest in curatorial studies, which is based more on a business model of performance than a creative model of investigation. With the continued expansion of the consumer upper class, the desire to be involved in the art world is often, and understandably, greater than the desire to question it. Art has become another collectible, another manifestation of class signification while increased museum attendance is less about an interest in art, per se, than a desire for an afternoon of entertainment with a sense of bettering oneself. The creative model that encourages chance-taking and celebrates failure as experiment and innovation is no longer an acceptable one to corporate funders and museum boards. Is the art world losing its sense of adventure and creativity or is the changing role of art responsible for its more controlled nature in many cases?

One's work in a creative field is autobiographical, a reflection of one's interests, values, and sensibilities. Identifying and understanding this connection is key to understanding the work, as the artist, author, or viewer. In discussions with curatorial students around the world, a major area of interest for me has been the disconnect between what really interests them and what they expect to do as curators. I have asked about what excites them and why. Why do they want to be curators? What do they see themselves doing in five years? The level of confusion is surprisingly and appropriately high. Within the institution the direction seems clear, but after leaving there is a kind of free fall. Many of these young curators tend to work with a relatively small group of artists and influences within a narrow range of defined issues. They don't venture outside the expected models of exhibition or relationships, or consider alternatives. This isn't because they aren't intelligent, quite the opposite. Many are extremely bright and this was the reason for their consternation. They aren't "getting it." And they aren't "getting" the real potential because in many programs they aren't being properly prepared, adequately challenged, or particularly well-educated. Often the readings tend to be superficial and disconnected, while discussions of practical issues such as fundraising and promotion take precedent over conceptual and ideological concerns. There are few classes or lectures about sociology, anthropology, or about contextualizing the readings, making it difficult to address larger issues. Too often this results in exhibition essays describing the work, quoting others, and engaging in classical obfuscation by using the kind of rhetoric that makes the insecure give credit to the writer rather than question the content.

It is interesting to consider whether curatorial programs might be better served if they were integrated into art history/art studies departments rather than operating as freestanding facilities or departments. Students would then better fill in historical and contextual areas not covered in the curatorial program syllabus. While students are told not to treat a curatorial program as a terminal degree, this is often the case, and we might consider whether we are fostering a profession that might be much more valuable and effective with additional training and study. As the mediator between the artist and the public, the non-affiliated curator could provide a valuable, challenging opportunity to all involved.

There are two discernible paths of direction emerging with curatorial programs. As noted, students and recent graduates often seem rather confused as they attempt to connect their program experience with the world outside. As a program focuses one's interests and practices, it can also narrow them as the willingness to risk is suppressed by greater competition and expectation. Familiar models develop to keep funding organizations from being surprised and the current manifestation of the independent curator model owes more to the power image of the corporate executive and less to the traditional academic. In control, well dressed, socially elevated, connected, and being needed. Art reflecting society's values. Fortunately there does seem to be some reassessment of this image and it remains to be seen whether it will affect the larger orientation.

One possible path is that of a facilitator, whose primary commitment is bringing art to the public. This may involve selecting the artist(s) and locating a venue, then organizing everything in the exhibition so that the art is presented per the artist's intent, largely in a non-critical advocacy role. In the artist selection process they decide what is good (what they like) and what is bad (what they don't like). They attend international events, doing more studio visits than the next person, giving them a sense of purpose, importance, belonging, and direction. The other and more compelling path is interested in wanting to understand the work and place it in a socio-cultural context in an attempt to understand and explain why the work was done, how it was done, what were the influences, the sociological and anthropological connections, and ideally to present it in a way that provides others entry and interest. Assessing how the work might be important or noteworthy, rather than good or bad.

The College Art Association began advising curatorial students more than a year ago that positions would not be available in the numbers needed, and certainly not in the major art centers where most want to be.

The desire to be a curator isn't enough, just as one's desire to be a writer doesn't make it happen. The potential of the profession is much greater than we accept, and it is up to each individual to determine what motivates him or her and why. Being creative is at times the easiest and the most difficult endeavor. It is mostly solitary by nature and lonely and cannot be taught. It can however be encouraged, guided, and directed by responsible educators and colleagues in an atmosphere of creative thinking and asking the questions that cause consideration. An institution is at its best when it encourages its staff to question its institutional structure. Success is being able to define and pursue the questions worthy of obsession and interest and to be able to maintain a lifelong interest in the pursuit.

Steven Rand is a working artist and practicing agonist. He founded apexart curatorial program in 1994 in response to a perceived "increase in commercialism and promotion at the expense of an emphasis on inquiry and creativity." His work is exhibited internationally with solo exhibitions in New York, Cologne, Buenos Aires and Shanghai, as well as many international group exhibitions. A permanent large-scale commission for the European Union Patent Office in Munich, Germany, was completed in 2005. Mr. Rand has spoken and lectured at the National College of Art and Design (Dublin), Rhode Island School of Design, Quarini Stamplia (Venice), Corcoran Museum, National Academy of Art (Vienna), School of Visual Arts, and University of Austin, CAAM Canary Islands, W139 (Amsterdam) University of Utrecht (Utrecht), Queens College, College Art Association, among others. More information available at www.stevenrand.info.

Heather Kouris

Introduction

What is the definition, evolution, and purpose of independent curatorial practice as compared to institutional engagement? Is the curator responsible for maintaining the integrity of the field with respect to promoting artists and advising? Is it the responsibility of independent curators to disseminate the culture of our times or are they held accountable for another specific direction? Do curatorial training programs adequately prepare graduates for the reality of administrative and funding duties required as an independent curator? *Cautionary Tales: Critical Curating* attempts to consider the changing role of the contemporary curator over the last decade. We invited ten diverse writers to address the questions above. Each author responded with what he or she felt were the relevant issues based on his or her various experiences.

How *has* the curator changed? The general working concept of the contemporary curator began in the 1960s when Harald Szeemann and Walter Hopps started working independently from institutions. Before that, art curators were always associated with an institution. Over the last ten or so years, curators have become an increasingly important player in the field of art. There are now no less than twenty curatorial training programs worldwide—from dedicated schools to specialized degrees in art history departments. The growing popularity and explosion of the curatorial profession means more training is necessary and more venues are incorporating the work of independent curators into their programs. The curator has also become much more "powerful" and has a stronger voice than ever before.

The authors of the essays included in *Cautionary Tales* each point in their own way to the important aspects of what it takes to be a "successful" curator. One main underlying concept of the essays is that curators must take risks in preparing their projects. A good exhibition is not merely a gathering of works of the fifty greatest artists, but should involve some reflection of societal input, and/or a certain recognition of art history, geography, and culture, not to mention sharing some sort of personal perspective. Those acting in the role of curator should be able to communicate their ideas or intentions easily and openly with the public who sees their exhibition.

David Levi Strauss reflects on the work and influence of Szeemann and Hopps and considers various models of curatorial possibility as well as the limitations imposed by the conservative institutions of the art world. He points to the essential attributes of curating, including the willingness to take greater chances and working against the bias of the world. Also using Szeemann and Hopps as primary examples of the first generation of contemporary curators, Kate Fowle explores how recent curatorial approaches respond to changes in art practice, as well as starting to establish its own vocabulary and status as a form in its own right. She shows how the art scene developed into a "dynamic and contradictory system" wherein the curator was released from the responsibilities of presiding over culture.

As Boris Groys emphasizes in his essay, artwork requires an exhibition and a curator to be seen; however, through his or her specific agenda, the curator often alters the significance of the artwork. His essay discusses the inherent value of an art object and the potential abuse the curator may inflict to art in terms of how the curator may change the meaning of art through its presentation. Rather than relying solely on the artwork's message, the curator reinterprets the artwork through the exhibition idea, thus taking the responsibility for the message of the exhibition. The changing approach of curatorial practice is discussed by Geeta Kapur through her examples from the 60s, 80s, 90s, and present day exhibitions to demonstrate how the contemporary curator works variously as a collaborator, an artwork co-producer, and a cultural critic, among other roles.

Sara Arrhenius, Young Chul Lee, and Dave Hickey address the inner workings of assembling biennial exhibitions through their specific experiences of biennial curating. Biennials begin with the ideal of bringing attention to a city, which places certain expectations on the invited curator by the biennial organizer. The curator must present a topic general enough to draw interest, but be interesting enough to survive the criticisms of the art world. Working as an external curator brings advantages as well as limitations. Sometimes biennials can result in homogenization, as Lee points out in his discussion of the "inter space" of cultural differences.

We learn also from the essays that the voice of the curator has begun to outweigh that of the critic. David Carrier presents many cases of the critic's voice not being heard as loudly as it once was. The critic may have had the tendency to "make or break" an artist; now it is the curator who appears to wield that power. The importance of curators being good writers is addressed in Andras Szanto's text; he uses an extended analogy between curating and editing—two enterprises faced with some similar challenges—to give advice to curators on how to approach exhibition making.

With so many training programs for people interested in the arts to learn "how to be a curator," it is important to consider the criteria used to ensure students understand what kind of responsibility curating entails. Finding the venue and writing a good essay are equally important parts of what the job requires. Jean-Hubert Martin gives advice on how to be a good independent curator based on his years of experience as a curator and administrator, including integrity and good communication.

Curators add a great deal to how artwork is viewed—they are not simply the "middle man" between the art and the viewer. Is there perhaps a way to ensure that curatorial practice maintains a high standard of exhibition making? Some professions have guidebooks or ethics guidelines. With the fast moving progression of how curators work, and the many variations of their practice—from large institutional curator to the artist as curator to curating a collection of books in a bookstore—it is nearly impossible to establish a one-size-fits-all way of working. There are also recent trends of artist as curator, critic as curator, and fashion designer as curator that make the profession seem somewhat of a free-for-all. Should there be standards for curatorial training programs to follow? Or would such standards put a shackle on the creative act?

While the essays in this book do not provide all the answers about the changing role of the contemporary curator nor exactly define the role of the curator, each one provides an interesting perspective and allows readers at every level of interest to pose their own questions and to find new answers.

Heather Kouris has been Special Projects Director of apexart since 2003; she was Gallery Director from 1999 to 2002. Now based in Athens, Greece, she continues her work with apexart and is developing work with the artistic community in Athens as well as writing about art. Her past curatorial efforts include *Everyday Hellas* (2004, White Box, NYC, and Parko Eleftherias, Athens) and *The Passions of the Good Citizen* (2002, apexart).

David Levi Strauss

The Bias of the World:
Curating After Szeemann & Hopps

What Is a Curator?

Under the Roman Empire, the title of curator ("caretaker") was given to officials in charge of various departments of public works: sanitation, transportation, policing. The *curatores annonae* were in charge of the public supplies of oil and corn. The *curatores regionum* were responsible for maintaining order in the fourteen regions of Rome. And the *curatores aquarum* took care of the aqueducts. In the Middle Ages, the role of the curator shifted to the ecclesiastical, as clergy who had a spiritual cure or charge. So one could say that the split within curating—between the management and control of public works (law) and the cure of souls (faith)—was there from the beginning. Curators have always been a curious mixture of bureaucrat and priest.

> That smooth-faced gentleman, tickling Commodity,
> Commodity, the bias of the world—
> —Shakespeare, *King John*[1]

For better or worse, curators of contemporary art have become, especially in the last ten years, the principal representatives of some of our most persistent questions and confusions about the social role of art. Is art a force for change and renewal, or is it a commodity, for advantage or convenience? Is art a radical activity, undermining social conventions, or is it a diverting entertainment for the wealthy? Are artists the antennae of the human race, or are they spoiled children with delusions of grandeur (in Roman law, a *curator* could also be the appointed caretaker or guardian of a minor or lunatic)? Are art exhibitions "spiritual undertakings with the power to conjure alternative ways of organizing society,"[2] or vehicles for cultural tourism and nationalistic propaganda?

These splits, which reflect larger tears in the social fabric, certainly in the United States, complicate the changing role of curators of contemporary art, because curators mediate between art and its publics and are often forced to take "a curving and indirect course" between them. Teaching for the past five years at the Center for Curatorial Studies at Bard College, I observed young curators confronting the practical demands and limitations of their profession, armed with a vision of possibility and an image of the curator as a free agent, capable of almost anything. Where did this image come from?

When Harald Szeemann and Walter Hopps died within a month of each other in February and March 2005, at age seventy-two and seventy-one, respectively, it was impossible not to see this as the end of an era. They were two of the principal architects of the present approach to curating contemporary art, working over fifty years to transform the practice. When young curators imagine what's possible, they are imagining (whether they know it or not) some version of Szeemann and Hopps. The trouble with taking these two as models of curatorial possibility is that both of them were *sui generis*: renegades who managed, through sheer force of will, extraordinary ability, brilliance, luck, and hard work, to make themselves indispensable, and thereby intermittently palatable, to the conservative institutions of the art world.

Each came to these institutions early. When Szeemann was named head of the Kunsthalle Bern in 1961, at age twenty-eight, he was the youngest ever to have been appointed to such a position in Europe, and when Hopps was made director of the Pasadena Art Museum (now the Norton Simon Museum) in 1964, at age thirty-one, he was then the youngest art museum director in the United States. By that time, Hopps (who never earned a college degree) had already mounted a show of paintings by Mark Rothko, Clyfford Still, Richard Diebenkorn, Jay DeFeo, and many others on a merry-go-round in an amusement park on the Santa Monica Pier (with his first wife, Shirley Hopps, when he was twenty-two); started and run two galleries (Syndell Studios and the seminal Ferus Gallery, with Ed Kienholz); and curated the first museum shows of Frank Stella's paintings and Joseph Cornell's boxes, the first U.S. retrospective of Kurt Schwitters, the first museum exhibition of Pop Art, and the first solo museum exhibition of Marcel Duchamp, in Pasadena in 1963. And that was just the beginning. Near the end of his life, Hopps estimated that he'd organized 250 exhibitions in his fifty-year career.

Szeemann's early curatorial activities were no less prodigious. He made his first exhibition, *Painters Poets/Poets Painters*, a tribute to Hugo Ball, in 1957, at age twenty-four. When he became the director of the Kunsthalle in Bern four years later, he completely transformed that institution, mounting nearly twelve exhibitions a year, culminating in the landmark show *Live In Your Head: When Attitudes Become Form*, in 1969, which exhibited works by seventy artists, including Joseph Beuys, Richard Serra, Eva Hesse, Lawrence Weiner, Richard Long, and Bruce Nauman, among many others.

While producing critically acclaimed and historically important exhibitions, both Hopps and Szeemann quickly came into conflict with their respective institutions. After four years at the Pasadena Art Museum, Hopps was asked to resign. He was named director of the Corcoran Gallery of Art in Washington, D.C. in 1970, then fired two years later. For his part, stunned by the negative reaction to *When Attitudes Become Form* from the Kunsthalle Bern, Harald Szeemann quit his job, becoming the first "independent curator." He set up the Agency for Spiritual Guestwork and co-founded the International Association of Curators of Contemporary Art (IKT) in 1969, curated *Happenings & Fluxus* at the Kunstverein in Cologne in 1970, and became the first artistic director of Documenta in 1972, reconceiving it as a 100-day event. Szeemann and Hopps hadn't yet turned forty, and their best shows were all ahead of them. For Szeemann, these included *Junggesellenmaschinen—Les Machines célibataires* ("Bachelor Machines") in 1975-77, "Monte Veritá" (1978, 1983, 1987), the first Aperto at the Venice Biennale (with Achille Bonito Oliva, 1980), *Der Hang Zum Gesamtkunstwerk, Europaïsche Utopien seit 1800* ("The Quest for the Total Work of Art") in 1983-84, *Visionary Switzerland* in 1991, the Joseph Beuys retrospective at the Centre Pompidou in 1993, *Austria in a Lacework of Roses* in 1996, and the Venice Biennale in 1999 and 2001. For Hopps, yet to come were exhibitions of Diane Arbus in the American pavilion at the Venice Biennale in 1972; the Robert Rauschenberg mid-career survey in 1976; retrospectives at the Menil Collection of Yves Klein, John Chamberlain, Andy Warhol, and Max Ernst; and exhibitions of Jay DeFeo (1990), Ed Kienholz (1996 at the Whitney), Rauschenberg again (1998), and James Rosenquist (2003 at the Guggenheim). Both Szeemann and Hopps had exhibitions open when they died—Szeemann's *Visionary Belgium*, for the Palais des Beaux-Arts in Brussels, and Hopps' George Herms retrospective at the Santa Monica Museum—and both had plans for many more exhibitions in the future.

What Do Curators Do?

Szeemann and Hopps were the Cosmas and Damian (or the Beuys and Duchamp) of contemporary curatorial practice. Rather than accepting things as they found them, they changed the way things were done. But finally, they will be remembered for only one thing: the quality of the exhibitions they made, for that is what curators do, after all. Szeemann often said he preferred the simple title of *Ausstellungsmacher* (exhibition-maker), but he acknowledged at the same time how many different functions this one job comprised: "administrator, amateur, author of introductions, librarian, manager and accountant, animator, conservator, financier, and diplomat." I have heard curators characterized at different times as:

Administrators
Advocates
Auteurs
Bricoleurs (Hopps' last show, the Herms retrospective, was titled *The Bricoleur of Broken Dreams ... One More Once*)
Brokers
Bureaucrats
Cartographers (Ivo Mesquita)
Catalysts (Hans Ulrich Obrist)
Collaborators
Cultural impresarios
Cultural nomads
Diplomats (When Bill Lieberman, who held top curatorial posts at both the Museum of Modern Art and the Metropolitan Museum of Art, died in May 2005, *Artnews* described him as "the consummate art diplomat.")

And that's just the beginning of the alphabet. When Hans Ulrich Obrist asked Walter Hopps to name important predecessors, the first one he came up with was Willem Mengelberg, the conductor of the New York Philharmonic, "for his unrelenting rigor." "Fine curating of an artist's work," he continued, "that is, presenting it in an exhibition—requires as broad and sensitive an understanding of an artist's work as a curator can possibly muster. This knowledge needs to go well beyond what is actually put in the exhibition....To me, a body of work by a given artist has an inherent kind of score that you try to relate to or understand. It puts you in a certain psychological state. I always tried to get as peaceful and calm as possible."[3]

But around this calm and peaceful center raged the "controlled chaos" of exhibition making. Hopps' real skills included an encyclopedic visual memory, the ability to place artworks on the wall and in a room in a way that made them sing,[4] the personal charm to get people to do things for him, and an extraordinary ability to look at a work of art and then account for his experience of it, and articulate this account to others in a compelling and convincing way.

It is significant, I think, that neither Szeemann nor Hopps considered himself a writer, but both recognized and valued good writing, and solicited and "curated" writers and critics as well as artists into their exhibitions and publications. Even so, many think the rise of the independent curator signaled the demise of criticism. In a recent article titled "Do Critics Still Matter?" Mark Spiegler opined that "on the day in 1969 when Harald Szeemann went freelance by leaving the Kunsthalle Bern, the wind turned against criticism."[5] There are curators who can also write criticism, but these precious few are the exceptions that prove the rule. Curators are not specialists, but for some reason they feel the need to use a specialized language, appropriated from philosophy or psychoanalysis, which too often obscures rather than reveals their sources and ideas. The result is not criticism, but *curatorial rhetoric*. Criticism involves making finer and finer distinctions among like things, while the inflationary writing of curatorial rhetoric is used to obscure fine distinctions with vague generalities. The latter's displacement of the former has political and social origins and effects, as we move into an increasingly managed, *post-critical* environment.

Although Szeemann and Hopps were very different in many ways, they shared certain fundamental values: an understanding of the importance of remaining independent of institutional prejudices and arbitrary power arrangements; a keen sense of history; the willingness to continually take risks intellectually, aesthetically, and conceptually; and an inexhaustible curiosity about and respect for the way artists work.

Szeemann's break from the institution of the Kunsthalle was, simply put, "a rebellion aimed at having more freedom."[6] This rebellious act put him closer to the ethos of artists and writers, in which authority must be earned through the quality of one's work. In his collaborations with artists, power relations were negotiated in practice rather than asserted as fiat. Every mature artist I know has a favorite horror story about a young, inexperienced curator trying to claim an authority he or she hasn't earned by manipulating a seasoned artist's work or by designing exhibitions in which individual artists' works are seen as secondary and subservient to the curator's grand plan or theme. The cure for this kind of insecure hubris is experience, but also the recognition of the ultimate contingency of the curatorial process. As Dave Hickey said of both critics and curators, "Somebody has to do something before we can do anything."[7] In June 2000, after being at the pinnacle of curatorial power repeatedly for over forty years, Harald Szeemann said, "Frankly, if you insist on power, then you keep going on in this way. But you must *throw the power away* after each experience, otherwise it's not renewing. I've done a lot of shows, but if the next one is not an adventure, it's not important for me and I refuse to do it."[8]

When contemporary curators, following in the steps of Szeemann, break free from institutions, they sometimes lose their sense of history in the process. Whatever their shortcomings, institutions do have a sense (sometimes a surfeit) of history. And without history, "the new" becomes a trap, a sequential recapitulation of past approaches with no forward movement. It is a terrible thing to be perpetually stuck in the present, and this is a major occupational hazard for curators.

Speaking about his curating of the Seville Biennale in 2004, Szeemann said, "It's not about presenting the best there is, but about discovering where the unpredictable path of art will go in the immanent future." But moving the ball up the field requires a tremendous amount of legwork. "The unpredictable path of art" becomes much less so when curators rely on the Claude Rains method, rounding up the usual suspects from the same well-worn list of artists that everyone else in the world is using.

It is difficult, in retrospect, to fully appreciate the risks that both Szeemann and Hopps took to change the way curators worked. One should never underestimate the value of a monthly paycheck. By giving up a secure position as director of a stable art institution and striking out on his own as an "independent curator," Szeemann was assuring himself years of penury. There was certainly no assurance that anyone would hire him as a freelance; anyone who's chosen this path knows that freelance means never having to say you're solvent. Being freelance as a writer and critic is one thing: the tools of the trade are relatively inexpensive, and one need only make a living. But making exhibitions is costly, and finding "independent" money, money without onerous strings attached to it, is especially difficult when one cannot, in good conscience, present it as an "investment opportunity." Daniel Birnbaum points out that "all the dilemmas of corporate sponsorship and branding in contemporary art today are fully articulated in [*When Attitudes Become Form*]. Remarkably, according to Szeemann, the exhibition came about only because 'people from Philip Morris and the PR firm Ruder Finn came to Bern and asked me if

I would do a show of my own. They offered me money and total freedom.' Indeed, the exhibition's catalog seems uncanny in its prescience: 'As businessmen in tune with our times, we at Philip Morris are committed to support the experimental,' writes John A. Murphy, the company's European president, asserting that his company experimented with 'new methods and materials' in a way fully comparable to the Conceptual artists in the exhibition. (And yet, showing the other side of this corporate-funding equation, it was a while before the company supported the arts in Europe again, perhaps needing time to recover from all the negative press surrounding the event.)"[9] So the founding act of "independent curating" was brought to you by ... Philip Morris! Thirty-three years later, for the Swiss national exhibition Expo.02, Szeemann designed a pavilion covered with sheets of gold, containing a system of pneumatic tubes and a machine that destroyed money—two one-hundred franc notes every minute during the 159 days of the exhibition. The sponsor? The Swiss National Bank, of course.

When Walter Hopps brought the avant-garde to Southern California, he didn't have to compete with others to secure the works of Mark Rothko, Clyfford Still, or Jay DeFeo (for the merry-go-round show in 1953), because no one else wanted them. In his Hopps obituary, *Los Angeles Times* critic Christopher Knight pointed out that "just a few years after Hopps' first visit to the [Arensbergs'] collection, the [Los Angeles] City Council decreed that modern art was Communist propaganda and banned its public display."[10] In fifty years, we've progressed from banning art as Communist propaganda to prosecuting artists as terrorists.[11]

The Few and Far Between

It's not that fast horses are rare,
but men who know enough to spot them
are few and far between.

—Han Yü[12]

The trait that Szeemann and Hopps had most in common was their respect for and understanding of artists. They never lost sight of the fact that their principal job was to take what they found in artists' works and do whatever it took to present it in the strongest possible way to an interested public. Sometimes this meant combining it with other work that enhanced or extended it. This was done not to show the artists anything they didn't already know, but to show the public. As Lawrence Weiner pointed out in an interview in 1994, "Everybody that was in the *Attitudes* show knew all about the work of everybody else in the *Attitudes* show. They wouldn't have known them personally, but they knew all the work.... Most artists on both sides of the Atlantic knew what was being done. European artists had been coming to New York and U.S. artists went over there."[13] But *Attitudes* brought it all together in a way that made a difference.

Both Szeemann and Hopps felt most at home with artists, sometimes literally. Carolee Schneemann recently described for me the scene in the Kunstverein in Cologne in 1970, when she and her collaborator in *Happenings and Fluxus* (having arrived and discovered there was no money for lodging) moved into their installations, and Szeemann thought it such a good idea to sleep on site, he brought in a cot and slept in the museum, to the outrage of the staff and guards. Both Szeemann and Hopps reserved their harshest criticism for the various bureaucracies that got between them and the artists. Hopps once described working for bureaucrats when he was a senior curator at the National Collection of Fine Arts as "like moving through an atmosphere of Seconal."[14] And Szeemann said in 2001 that "the annoying thing about such bureaucratic organizations at the [Venice] Biennale is that there are a lot of people running around who hate artists because they keep running around wanting to change everything."[15] Changing everything, for Szeemann, was just the point. "Artists, like curators, work on their own," he said in 2000, "grappling with their attempt to make a world in which to survive.... We are lonely people, faced with superficial politicians, with donors, sponsors, and one must deal with all of this. I think it is here where the artist finds a way to form his own world and live his obsessions. *For me, this is the real society.*"[16] The society of the obsessed.

Where Do We Go from Here?

Although Walter Hopps was an early commissioner for the São Paolo Biennal (1965: Barnett Newman, Frank Stella, Richard Irwin, and Larry Poons) and of the Venice Biennale (1972: Diane Arbus), Harald Szeemann practically invented the role of nomadic independent curator of huge international shows, putting his indelible stamp on Documenta and Venice and organizing the Lyon Biennale and the Kwangju Biennial in Korea in 1997, and the first Seville Biennale in 2004, as well as numerous other international surveys around the world.

So what Szeemann said about globalization and art should perhaps be taken seriously. He saw globalization as a euphemism for imperialism, and proclaimed that "globalization is the great enemy of art." And in the Carolee Thea interview in 2000, he said, "Globalization is perfect if it brings more justice and equality to the world ... but it doesn't. Artists dream of using computer or digital means to have contact and to bring continents closer. But once you have the information, it's up to you what to do with it. Globalization without roots is meaningless in art."[17] And globalization of the curatorial class can be a way to avoid or "transcend" the political.

Rene Dubos's old directive to "think globally, but act locally" (first given at the United Nations Conference on the Human Environment in 1972) has been upended in some recent international shows (like the 14th Sydney Biennale in 2004 and the first 1st Moscow Biennial in 2005). When one thinks locally (within a primarily Euro-American cultural framework, or within a New York-London-Kassel-Venice-Basel-Miami framework) but acts globally, the results are bound to be problematic, and can be disastrous. In 1979, Dubos argued for an ecologically sustainable world in which "natural and social units maintain or recapture their identity, yet interplay with each other through a rich system of communications." At their best, the big international exhibitions do contribute to this. Okwui Enwezor's[18] Documenta XI certainly did, and Szeemann knew it. At their worst, they perpetuate the center-to-periphery hegemony and preclude real cross-cultural communication and change. Although having artists and writers move around in the world is an obvious good, real cultural exchange is something that must be nurtured. Walter Hopps said in 1996: "I really believe in—and, obviously, hope for—radical, or arbitrary, presentations, where cross-cultural and cross-temporal considerations are extreme, out of all the artifacts we have. ... So just in terms of people's priorities, conventional hierarchies begin to shift some."[19]

The Silence of Szeemann & Hopps Is Overrated

'Art' is any human activity that aims at producing improbable situations,
and it is the more artful (artistic) the less probable the situation that it produces.
—Vilém Flusser[20]

Harald Szeemann recognized early and long appreciated the utopian aspects of art. "The often-evoked 'autonomy' is just as much a fruit of subjective evaluation as the ideal society: it remains a utopia while it informs the desire to experientially visualize the *unio mystica* of opposites in space. Which is to say that without seeing, there is nothing visionary, but that the visionary should always determine the seeing." And he recognized that the bureaucrat could overtake the curer of souls at any point. "Otherwise, we might just as well return to 'hanging and placing,' and divide the entire process 'from the vision to the nail' into detailed little tasks again."[21] He organized exhibitions in which the improbable could occur, and was willing to risk the impossible. In reply to a charge that the social utopianism of Joseph Beuys was never realized, Szeemann said, "The nice thing about utopias is precisely that they fail. For me failure is a poetic dimension of art."[22] Curating a show in which nothing could fail was, to Szeemann, a waste of time.

If he and Hopps could still encourage young curators in anything, I suspect it would be to take greater risks in their work. At a time when all parts of the social and political spheres (including art institutions) are increasingly *managed*, breaking out of this frame, asking significant questions, and setting the terms of resistance is more and more vitally important. It is important to work against the bias of the world (commodity, political expediency). For curators of contemporary art, that means finding and supporting those artists who, as Flusser writes, "have attempted, at the risk of their lives, to utter that which is unutterable, to render audible that which is ineffable, to render visible that which is hidden."[23]

1. Shakespeare, *The Life and Death of King John*, Act II, Scene 1, 573-74. Cowper: "What Shakespeare calls commodity, and we call political expediency." Appendix 13 of my old edition of Shakespeare's *Complete Works*, edited by G. B. Harrison (NY: Harcourt, Brace & World, 1968), pp. 1639-40, reads: "Shakespeare frequently used poetic imagery taken from the game of bowls [bowling].... The bowl [bowling ball] was not a perfect sphere, but so made that one side somewhat protruded. This protrusion was called the *bias*; it caused the bowl to take a curving and indirect course."
2. "When Attitude Becomes Form: Daniel Birnbaum on Harald Szeemann," *Artforum*, Summer 2005, p. 55.
3. Hans Ulrich Obrist, *Interviews, Volume 1* edited by Thomas Boutoux (Milan: Edizioni Charta, 2003), pp. 416-17. Hopps also named as predecessors exhibition-makers Katherine Dreier, Alfred Barr, James Johnson Sweeney, René d'Harnoncourt, and Jermayne MacAgy.
4. In 1976, at the Museum of Temporary Art in Washington, D.C., Hopps announced that, for thirty-six hours, he would hang anything anyone brought in, as long as it would fit through the door. Later, he proposed to put 100,000 images up on the walls of P.S. 1 in New York, but that project was, sadly, never realized.
5. Mark Spiegler, "Do Art Critics Still Matter?" *The Art Newspaper*, no. 157, April 2005, p. 32.
6. Carolee Thea, *Foci: Interviews with Ten International Curators* (New York: Apex Art Curatorial Program, 2001), p. 19.
7. *Curating Now: Imaginative Practice/Public Responsibility: Proceedings from a symposium addressing the state of current curatorial practice organized by the Philadelphia Exhibitions Initiative, October 14-15, 2000*, edited by Paula Marincola (Philadelphia: Philadelphia Exhibitions Initiative, 2001), p. 128. Both Szeemann and Hopps passed Hickey's test: "The curator's job, in my view," he said, "is to tell the truth, to show her or his hand, and get out of the way" (p. 126).

8. Thea, p. 19 (emphasis added).

9. Birnbaum, p. 58.

10. Christopher Knight, "Walter Hopps, 1932-2005. Curator Brought Fame to Postwar L.A. Artists," *Los Angeles Times*, March 22, 2005.

11. At this writing, the U.S. government continues in its effort to prosecute artist and University at Buffalo professor Steven Kurtz for obtaining bacterial agents through the mail, even though the agents were harmless and intended for use in art pieces by the collaborative Critical Art Ensemble. Kurtz has said he believes the charges filed against him in 2004 (after agents from the FBI, the Joint Terrorism Task Force, the Department of Homeland Security, and the Department of Defense swarmed over his house) are part of a Bush administration campaign to prevent artists from protesting government policies. "I think we're in a very unfortunate moment now in U.S. history," Kurtz has said. "A form of neo-McCarthyism has made a comeback.... We're going to see a whole host of politically motivated trials which have nothing to do with crime but everything to do with artistic expression." For the latest developments in the Kurtz case, go to caedefensefund.org.

12. Epigraph to Nathan Sivin's *Chinese Alchemy: Preliminary Studies* (Cambridge, MA: Harvard University Press, 1968).

13. *Having Been Said: Writings & Interviews of Lawrence Weiner 1968-2003*, edited by Gerti Fietzek and Gregor Stemmrich (Ostfildern-Ruit: Hatje Cantz Verlag, 2004), p. 315.

14. Hans Ulrich Obrist, "Walter Hopps Hopps Hopps—Art Curator," *Artforum*, February 1996.

15. Jan Winkelman, "Failure as a Poetic Dimension: A Conversation with Harald Szeemann," *Metropolis M. Tijdschrift over Hedendaagse Kunst*, No. 3, June 2001.

16. Thea, p. 17 (emphasis added).

17. Thea, p. 18.

18. With his co-curators Carlos Basualdo, Uta Meta Bauer, Susanne Ghez, Sarat Maharaj, Mark Nash, and Octavio Zaya.

19. Obrist, p. 430.

20. Vilém Flusser, "Habit: The True Aesthetic Criterion," in *Writings*, edited by Andreas Ströhl, translated by Erik Eisel (Minneapolis and London: University of Minnesota Press, 2002), p. 52.

21. Harald Szeemann, "Does Art Need Directors?" in *Words of Wisdom: A Curator's Vade Mecum on Contemporary Art*, edited by Carin Kuoni (New York: Independent Curators International, 2001), p. 169.

22. Winkelman.

23. Flusser, p. 54.

David Levi Strauss's collection of essays on photography and politics, *Between the Eyes*, with an introduction by John Berger, has been released in paperback by Aperture, and in a new Italian edition by Postmedia, and *Between Dog & Wolf: Essays on Art and Politics* was published by Autonomedia in 1999. He taught at the Center for Curatorial Studies at Bard College from 2001-2005, and now teaches in the MFA program in studio art at Bard College.

Kate Fowle

Who cares?
Understanding the Role of the Curator Today

The curator is having an identity crisis. Curating is now an industry, constructing its own histories as it evolves. At the same time, it is an increasingly multifaceted practice that gives rise to much speculation as to how it functions and what it entails.

In the opening paragraph of an essay intended as advice to a new generation of curators, Harald Szeemann suggests we look to the root of the word, which is *curare*, meaning "to take care of." He writes, "After all, the word curator already contains the concept of care."[1] But what is this seemingly inevitable "concept" that Szeemann is referring to? It has a number of implications that influence how the role of the curator is understood.

While the word stemmed from the Latin, in English it evolved to mean "guardian" or "overseer." From 1362 "curator" was used to signify people who cared for (or were in superintendence of) minors or lunatics, and in 1661 it began to denote "one in charge of a museum, library, zoo or other place of exhibit."[2] In each case it has hierarchical connotations—a curator is someone who presides *over* something—suggesting an inherent relationship between care and control.

This is not uncharted territory. Michel Foucault, for example, has extensively explored how this and other meanings of care have developed. In his book *Madness and Civilization*, he describes the Hôpital Général in Paris as a 17th century institution that was not a medical establishment, but a house of confinement for those deemed insane. Rather than being a place of protection and aid, he suggests that it was "a sort of semi judicial structure, an administrative entity which, along with the already constituted powers, and outside of the courts, decides, judges and executes."[3] Similarly, the operations of a public gallery or museum could historically be understood to be as much about the administration and governing of culture as about a concern for its preservation and presentation.

Many public museums were initially funded and run by the government or state, and curators were therefore civil servants, working in the service of politicians and bureaucrats. In the United Kingdom, at least, some of the first local art museums were created to bestow care on the people, using art as a pedagogical tool. In a newspaper report written in May 1892 about the opening of a public museum in Walsall (a small industrial town in the west Midlands), the journalist quotes extensively from the mayor's inaugural speech, which started with an explanation of how societal developments indicated that the council could no longer be content with restricting civic duties to "maintaining law and order, and preventing people from dying of starvation." The gallery—filled with paintings and objects borrowed from local dignitaries—was instigated because it was time to "look after the popular culture of the masses." The journalist went on to describe how the mayor was met with great applause when he suggested that "the manners of the people would become softer and less uncouth" when they stood before art. He also predicted that the workers would be "cheered and instructed and lifted to a higher level" as a result of their experience.[4]

In this ceremonious display of generosity, exhibition-making is given a charitable sense of social responsibility. In other circumstances the impetus is more ideological, with art used as propaganda. This is evident in footage of the 1917 October Revolution in Russia, which documents the trains that were used as mobile exhibitions, dispatched across the country to give word of the revolution to the peasants. Here, carriages were adorned with artists' romanticized visions of the worker and filled with slogans and images that illustrated a new world order.

While its politics were markedly different, after its assumption to power, the Nazi Party built museums and used exhibitions to control the dissemination of culture. Perhaps the most famous example is the *Entartete Kunst* (Degenerate Art) exhibition that opened in Munich in 1937, which was initiated as an official condemnation of modern art that promoted morals the public was *not* encouraged to embrace.[5] The magnitude of the Nazi's convictions only served to reveal the depth of their anxiety, a condition that is generally recognized as both a source and a by-product of caring.

Over 650 paintings, sculptures, prints and books that had been confiscated from thirty-two state-run museums were hung chaotically in the cramped second-floor confines of the former Institute of Archaeology. Rooms were themed to highlight how artists had demeaned aspects of society such as religion and women, or were dedicated to "degenerate" styles, such as Dada, abstraction and Expressionism. Throughout the exhibition, artworks were interspersed with slogans such as "Nature as seen by sick minds," or "An insult to German heroes of the Great War," as well as signs that revealed how much money the previous government had paid for such abominations. In all probability the majority of visitors were intrigued by the spectacle, rather than educated on the virtues of racial purity, as was the intention. Either way, the exhibition went down in history as the first (and probably the only free) block-buster of modern art—it is generally recorded as the most highly attended show in the 20th century.

With the charge of researching, acquiring, documenting, and publicly displaying art, the curator becomes the propagator of taste and knowledge for the public "good." It stands to reason, then, that during this process one must also have the opportunity to further refine oneself. This is the give and take of generosity. In this respect care takes on a reciprocal value, rather than just being an act of dubious kindness or concern. The curator becomes a connoisseur as much as an administrator. His or her role is expanded beyond "overseeing" to encompass what Foucault calls "the cultivation of the self."

He explains that from Ancient Greek times, this was practiced between small social groups that were "bearers of culture," who understood that the "art of existence" could have meaning and worth if one followed the principle of taking "care of oneself." He describes it as involving the adoption of an approach to life that used "procedures, practices, and formulas that people reflected on, developed, perfected and taught. It thus came to constitute a social practice, giving rise to relationships between individuals, to exchanges and communications, and at times even to institutions."[6] It could be said that several modern museums, including the Museum of Modern Art in New York, developed under such conditions, as a socialized process of self-fulfillment for those who brought it into existence.

Founded in 1929, the museum was privately funded and governed by a board of trustees who were all connoisseurs, if not professionally active in the field. Alfred H. Barr Jr. became the first director at the age of 27. His curatorial approach was influenced by his education at Princeton and Harvard and his travels in Europe and Russia. In particular, at Harvard he was introduced to the Fogg Method, which included museology, as well as courses that focused on physical attributes and the syntax of the work of art, rather than the social and psychological contexts of the form.

Throughout his tenure, Barr's motivation was academic, as opposed to civic or political. He was less concerned with "improving" the public than with proving the merits of the formal qualities of modern art to critics, collectors, artists and philanthropists. Upholding both the self-cultivation and the control in Foucault's descriptions of care, Barr used the sanctity of the white cube to produce exhibitions that elevated the "autonomous object." Becoming one of the first well known, or celebrity, curators, he was heralded for major contributions to the study of modern art and established many artists' careers in the process. But although Barr respected and was influenced by artists, architects, and designers, his practice was still one that promoted his own knowledge and opinions over theirs.

For the most part, it was during the 1950s that there was a significant shift in these relationships of power in Europe and the United States, with the rise of artist-led initiatives in establishing venues and forums for art. For example, in New York a number of artists' collectives started accumulating around Tenth Street in Greenwich Village, such as the Hansa Gallery, founded in 1952, by students of Hans Hoffman, including Jean Follet, Allan Kaprow, and George Segal. What each gallery had in common was that the curatorial role was taken on by artist committees, leveling the hierarchical model of exhibition-making.

In London, the Independent Group transformed the audience from a spectator into a participant in the production of culture. Consisting of artists, architects, and critics—Richard Hamilton, Alison and Peter Smithson, and Lawrence Alloway, to name a few—the group developed around the Institute of Contemporary Art from 1952, providing a forum for public debate through lectures, dialogues, and exhibitions. Its project aimed to be anti-elitist and anti-academic, discussing art as part of a communication network that also included movies, advertising, fashion, and product design.

Such activities signaled the evolution of the art scene into a dynamic and contradictory system. Just as curating exhibitions was no longer only the domain of the museum professional, audiences weren't a faceless public, devoid of the people who were the makers of culture. Through the deviances that rapidly developed from that time on—such as museums acknowledging the voice of the artist, or artist-led galleries employing exhibition organizers—the function of the curator was potentially released from charitable responsibilities and the service of power. Open to reinterpretation, the role became more flexible and therefore also more vulnerable.

These were the conditions under which Harald Szeemann began to make exhibitions. Although he is now generally acknowledged as the first "independent" curator, he also appropriated the concept of care from the conventional root of the profession, as we have established. Along with others of his generation, such as

Walter Hopps, he understood curating as more intricate than presenting art in relation to the mandate of an institution.

From the mid-50s on, Szeemann and Hopps each developed practices that have greatly influenced how the curator and exhibition-making are perceived today.[7] Both also died early in 2005, signifying closure on an era of major transformation in cultural production. While their characters and careers were markedly different, they shared a desire to challenge the bureaucracy of institutions, earning reputations for actively questioning the form of exhibitions as well as for their sustained engagement with artists and their work.

In 1969, as director of the Kunsthalle Bern in Switzerland, Szeemann initiated *Live in Your Head: When Attitudes Become Form: Works-Processes-Concepts-Situations-Information*, an exhibition that turned the gallery into a studio, with artists traveling to Bern to produce installations and actions that extended into the city streets. Recognizing new art forms that were developing under terms such as earth art, concept art, anti-form and arte povera, the show included projects by nearly seventy artists, including Joseph Beuys, Michael Heizer, Eva Hesse, Mario Merz, Allen Ruppersberg and Robert Smithson. *Attitudes* marked the advent of the contemporary curatorial drive, what Bruce Altshuler calls "the rise of the curator as creator," whereby exhibition organizing became a critical and potentially experimental endeavor.[8] Shortly after the show, Szeemann left the Kunsthalle (where the trustees largely disagreed with his methods) and developed projects for a variety of museums, galleries and biennials, as well as for quasi-private and non-gallery spaces. From this point his practice focused on the concept of exhibition-making as an ongoing process that was separate from the programmatic functions of an institution. Becoming in effect the precursor to the "frequent-flyer," "nomadic," or "itinerant" curator, Szeemann instigated a number of curatorial models that we now take for granted.

For example, as the director of *Documenta 5* in 1972, he challenged the established premise that the quinquennial take the form of a temporary museum, introducing instead the concept of the exhibition as a live project, or a hundred-day event. In this context he organized performances, happenings, and films under sub-themes that considered works in relation to science fiction, advertising and utopian design, as well as inviting artists to present their own museums and political statements. In 1980, as co-commissioner for the Venice Biennale, Szeemann introduced the Aperto[9]—a themed, international group exhibition for emerging artists— which transcended the national divisions of the pavilions. This lasting intervention into the structure of the Biennale asserted his long-held belief that exhibitions did not have to be conceptually or qualitatively conclusive, but rather could act as a testing ground for artists and a barometer for the development of art practice.

Walter Hopps never completed a formal education. He started out working with musicians in the Los Angeles jazz scene, which influenced his ideas on how to help artists give a public presence to their work. Then he set up the Ferus Gallery in 1957 with artist Ed Keinholz, which would be the first platform in Los Angeles for international post-war art, as well as for unknown beat-generation and West Coast artists such as Wallace Berman, Jay DeFeo, and Georg Herms. Conceived of in the spirit of an artists' collective, within a year the gallery had developed into a successful commercial (although still experimental) enterprise under the leadership of Irvine Blum, establishing a financially driven momentum that remains a contested aspect (or perhaps a sub-plot) of exhibition-making.

Known as a perfectionist and nonconformist who refused to submit to the administrative logic or routine of the institution, Hopps nevertheless worked for a series of museums and biennials, while sustaining an interest in developing projects outside the gallery or museum setting. At the time of his death he was an art editor for the literary arts journal *Grand Street*, and also served as an adjunct senior curator at New York's Solomon R. Guggenheim Museum, as well holding the position of senior curator of 20th century art at the Menil Collection in Houston.

While it is possible to cite a number of important group shows curated by Hopps, what is potentially most interesting about his practice is his expansion of the parameters of solo shows by living artists. He curated Marcel Duchamp's first retrospective in 1963 (arranging two live chess matches for Duchamp as part of the show) and developed presentations of the work of Joseph Cornell, Barnett Newman, Robert Rauschenberg, and Kurt Schwitters, to name but a few. In an interview with curator Hans Ulrich Obrist, Hopps said, "To me, a body of work by a given artist has an inherent kind of score that you try to relate to or understand. It puts you in a certain psychological state." His practice involved ongoing research into conducive ways to present art: "Fine curating of an artist's work—that is, presenting it in an exhibition— requires as broad and sensitive understanding of an artist's work as a curator can possibly muster. This knowledge needs to go well beyond what is actually put in the exhibition."[10]

This philosophy underpinned his role at the Menil Collection, where he became the founding director in 1979, at a time when Dominique de Menil wanted to extend the feeling of intimacy that she had with her collection into its public display. Likening the experience to working in a research laboratory—in terms of how the artworks were commissioned, acquired, and presented—Hopps championed the potential of museum spaces as places of discovery, surprise, and contemplation.

The actions and attitudes of both Szeeman and Hopps highlight key factors in curating today: namely, that it provides a platform for artists' ideas and interests; it should be responsive to the situations in which it occurs; and it should creatively address timely artistic, social, cultural or political issues. It could be said that the role of the curator has shifted from a governing position that presides over taste and ideas to one that lies *amongst* art (or object), space, and audience. The motivation is closer to the experimentation and inquiry of artists' practices than to the academic or bureaucratic journey of the traditional curator.

Given that their careers began as the curatorial climate was changing, it is relevant to note that neither Szeemann nor Hopps called themselves curators at the outset. Hopps frequently likened his practice to that of a conductor, and Szeemann often chose to use the title *Ausstellungsmacher*, or exhibition-maker, describing this role as one of an "administrator, amateur, author of introductions, librarian, manager and accountant, animator, conservator, financier, and diplomat."[11] Indeed, it is only relatively recently that the use of the word *curator* in this contemporary context has gone mainstream; as awareness has grown, so has the proliferation of specialist articles, interviews, books, symposia, and graduate courses.

These have accumulated for the last decade, forming a critical frame-work through which exhibitions—as opposed to artworks—are given a kind of autonomy. Predominantly generated from within the field, the commentaries are indicative of the continuing self-reflexive aspect of the curatorial role. In working between theory and practice, the curator is simultaneously initiating, supporting, disseminating, and evaluating projects. This differs from the production of meaning that has developed around art, which is mostly generated by schools of art history and critical theory that exist alongside art practice.

Updating Szeemann's description of exhibition-maker, we can now add mediator, facilitator, middleman, and producer to the ever-expanding list of roles. Instead of comparing the curator to a conductor, as Hopps did, we live in an age when the curator is compared to a DJ, or any similar master of improvisation who "samples" and combines works, actions, and ideas. The institution is now not just the museum, but a whole industry that has grown up around exhibition-making. This situation has parallels with that described by Rosalind Krauss in her essay "Sculpture in the Expanded Field," first published in *October* in 1979, when new forms of art practice (such as those that Szeemann and Hopps supported) were increasingly being recognized. In the beginning of her text she writes:

> Over the last ten years rather surprising things have come to be called sculpture: narrow corridors with TV monitors at the ends; large photographs documenting country hikes; mirrors placed at strange angles in ordinary rooms; temporary lines cut into the floor of the desert. Nothing, it would seem, could possibly have given way to such a motley effort to lay claim to whatever one might mean by the category of sculpture. Unless, that is, the category can be made to become almost infinitely malleable.[12]

If we replace the word *sculpture* with *exhibition*, this could equally read as a commentary on recent forms of curatorial practice. Taking this further, we can replace Krauss's list of "surprising things" with recent examples of exhibitions, to see how far the term has been stretched. These could include: twenty-six days of live and Web-streamed radio broadcasts; artworks that can be touched, used and taken from the display; a human-scale live jungle installed alongside a laughing-gas chamber; mobile units, performances, outdoor museums and film screenings sited in the desert. Of course, such a list could take many forms, but by echoing Krauss we can readily establish that contemporary exhibitions are now not only dealing with the presentation of an expanded notion of art, but also extending their own spatial parameters into conceptual and virtual realms, as well as experimenting with the role of the public in the "completion" of a project.

Furthermore, as Szeemann and Hopps demonstrated, actively engaging with art and artists is central to practice, which is an aspect of the role for which there are no guarantees of immediate or quantifiable outcomes. This requires a kind of creative "maintenance," as opposed to Foucault's "care," as it involves supporting the seeds of ideas, sustaining dialogues, forming and reforming opinions, and continuously updating research. It could also be said that exhibitions are not the first, or only, concern of the curator. Increasingly the role includes producing commissioned temporary artworks, facilitating residencies, editing artist-books, and organizing one-time events.

In her essay, Krauss describes how "critical operations," such as art history and criticism, have historicized artists' practices so as to invent a virtually seamless trajectory for the development of sculpture from its "historically bound" category.

In contrast, rather than trying to smooth over the "ruptures" that have taken place in the field, she recognizes that they are a symptom of the breakdown within changing cultural conditions of the logic of the original definition. As a result, she charts the theoretical structure of an expanded field of sculpture that acknowledges the inconsistencies and transgressions.

Within contemporary curating the contradictions are evident to all. There is a widening divide between two camps—the independent and the institutional—that supposedly signifies where curatorial allegiances lie in relation to the "historically bound" aspects of the profession. These categorizations are overly simplistic, giving rise to restrictive perceptions of the role of the curator, even among those working in the field. Following Krauss's lead, we need to complicate the dialectics and acknowledge the diversity of practices that continue to develop around artists and their ideas. We need to start thinking in terms of an expanded field of curating.

1. Harald Szeemann, "Does Art Need Directors?" in *Words of Wisdom: A Curator's Vade Mecum on Contemporary Art*, edited by Carin Kuoni, (New York: Independent Curators International, 2001), p. 167.
2. These definitions are taken from the *On-line Etymology Dictionary*, Douglas Harper (www.etymonline.com, 2001). In cross-referencing *The Barnhart Concise Dictionary of Etymology*, edited by Robert K. Barnhart (New York: Harper Resource, an imprint of Harper Collins Publishers, 1995) p. 178-179, more incarnations of the word are found. From around 1375 "curature" is a person having the care of souls.
3. Michel Foucault, *Madness and Civilization: A History of Insanity in the Age of Reason*, translated by Richard Howard (New York: Vintage Books Edition, Random House, 1988), p. 40.
4. *Walsall Observer* May 21, 1892. The article was transcribed and archived by the Walsall Historical Society and the journalist's name was not recorded.
5. Max Nordau first developed the theory of degeneracy in 1892 in his book *Entartung* (Degeneration) where he used pseudoscientific reasoning to suggest that modern art movements such as Symbolism and Impressionism were the result of artists experiencing mental pathology and having a diseased visual cortex. The Nationalist Social Party adopted Nordau's theories during the Weimar Republic in Germany.
6. Michel Foucault, *The Care of the Self*. Volume 3 of *The History of Sexuality*, translated by Robert Hurley (New York: Vintage Books, Random House, 1988), p. 45.
7. Harald Szeemann died February 18, 2005, in the Ticino region of Switzerland, at the age of seventy-one. Walter Hopps died March 20, 2005, in Los Angeles, at the age of seventy-two.
8. Bruce Altshuler, *The Avant-Garde in Exhibition: New Art in the 20th Century* (Berkeley and Los Angeles: University of California Press, 1998), p. 236. Of the curator as creator, Altshuler goes on to say: "While there had been many earlier attempts to subvert the traditional exhibition format, these efforts were made by artists themselves. ... In the late sixties exhibition forms proliferated, but major innovations would also be generated by exhibition organizers. Like the work displayed, their exhibitions sought to undercut the standard way of framing art for the public, the manner and mode of presentation becoming part of the content presented. In this way they were engaged in the same sort of critical enterprise as the artists, and their exhibitions became works on a par with their components."
9. The first *Aperto* section for young artists at the Venice Biennale was arranged by Achille Bonito Oliva and Harald Szeemann in the Magazzini del Sale. It was at the 48th International Art Exhibition in 1999, when Szeeman was director, that the *Aperto* was first presented throughout the historical spaces of the Arsenale, growing to the hyper-large exhibition that we know today.

10. Hans Ulrich Obrist, "Walter Hopps Hopps Hopps—art curator," *Artforum*, February 1996.

11. Obrist, ibid.

12. Rosalind Krauss's "Sculpture in the Expanded Field" was originally published in *October* 8 (Spring 1979); reprinted in *The Anti-Aesthetic: Essays on Post-modern Culture*, edited and with an introduction by Hal Foster (New York: New Press, 1998), p. 31-42.

Thanks to Julian Myers for discussing and commenting on the ideas that are developed in this essay.

Kate Fowle is the Chair of the MA Program in Curatorial Practice at California College of the Arts in San Francisco, and an independent curator and writer. Currently she is working on *The Backroom*, an ongoing research project into artists' source materials, which recently occupied a space in Culver City, L.A., (2005). Texts and publications include *What We Want Is Free: Generosity and Exchange in Recent Art*, edited by Ted Purves (SUNY Press, NY, 2005) and *Flow: Ari Marcopoulos* (MU, Eindhoven, 2006).

Jean-Hubert Martin

Independent Curatorship

The main task of an independent curator is to conceive and organize exhibitions, which includes also the editing of catalogs. He is the go-between among the different worlds of the artists, the exhibition spaces (gallery, museum, etc.), and the public. By showing art and writing about it, the curator interprets the works and conveys his understanding to the viewers. Consequently the independent curator can lead the visitor to new considerations or interpretations about art. This might open up new trends. The curator must be aware of different types of public: On one hand there are the amateurs who know the codes of art already; on the other hand there is the visitor who is inexperienced in contemporary art and wants to discover it.

In terms of curating there is a big difference between personal exhibitions and group exhibitions. In the last case—group exhibitions—the role of an independent curator is best shown and visible. He gathers artists to give the visitor a sensation and idea of a common denominator that has to be easily verified in each work. This common link can either be formal or conceptual. On the other hand a personal exhibition allows the independent curator to interpret the work of one artist according to his personal perspective and setting the artists into new associations.

Independent curators work for either private or public institutions. They are actually sought out because experiencing the newest trends and the last innovations in the world of art requires gathering an enormous amount of information. Therefore a lot of travelling is required, and most curators who are tied to one institution are unable to find enough time for travelling. Information can of course easily be gathered through publications, i.e., art magazines or the internet, but direct contacts with artists and their works is essential to understand and to feel the quality and the energy that are inherent in the works. This applies to relatively conventional works of art, especially those with a physical or material presence.

The situation is different for more experimental or social works that are displayed within an urban context. Ephemeral works or interactive works require much more involvement by intermediaries like independent curators. In this case the independent curator has often to look for an institutional partner, not necessarily a museum, that he can persuade to present the project. He has to identify the right place, where those who are responsible for the program are not only convinced by the artistic and aesthetic value of the work, but are also willing to raise the needed money. Such a situation is most closely comparable to organizing a festival of performance art.

Actually there is an artistic tendency in producing not just transportable paintings and sculptures but also ephemeral works *in situ*. Looking at this evolution it seems quite clear that more and more artists propose sets of social games, creating in cities situations of surprise or of self-consciousness and self-reflection. This seems to be a very attractive movement for many young artists. Thus they escape the necessity of producing objects for the market and they can enjoy a much greater freedom —at least at the beginning of their career. It is a paradox that the old request of artists of the 1960s, then in a Marxist context, is happening now through the evolution of society and multiple sources of financing. A few years ago, there were just a few regular contemporary art events, which were reserved, de facto, for a well-off public that was sufficiently interested to make the journey to Venice or Kassel. It is natural, and a good thing, that this situation should have been turned around, that art should move to the public. Around the world, the major events are becoming more numerous, thus providing greater possibilities of access to current creative activity. With the propagation of exhibition venues (at least one new museum opens each month) the progressive extension of the contemporary art network over the entire planet is profoundly transforming the situation and conditions of creative work. Today a range of artists are able to survive from their work with museums, exhibitions, grants, artist in residence programs, public art projects, workshops, lectures, etc. That is what the artists of the 60s required: freedom and independence from the art market, so that they were no longer obliged to produce their art for sale.

This evolution leads to the fact that the works of living artists are often ephemeral. The so-called crisis in art really only exists in the mind of those observers who are still trying to assign art with rules and limits to which the artists themselves are in fact totally indifferent. Although the creation itself is a result of the artist's individual crisis, its social diffusion seems to increase recently. The idea of an avant-garde, which has long been criticized for turning into the exclusive criterion of an autonomous microcosm, that has its nose stuck in its own *Guinness Book of Records*, is at last in the process of flying apart. The adventure of the world of living art, open to cultures as a whole, corresponds to a change in attitude that is perceptible today among many creative artists. What is appearing now is a profusion of works aimed at giving an account of the real: its ambiguities, its contradictions and its blind spots. This current grew up out of observations of a reality in full-scale evolution, and not out of the dogma of modernity. The generation of today's artists flees weightiness and monumentality. It tackles humanity's problems with vivacity, energy, and, indeed, humor; which means that it has avoided any trace of complex about the modernity from which it has freed itself. What unites the artists of this generation is a rejection of conventions as undeniable truths, whether denominational and philosophical or social and political. The critical function of the work of art, which has already been squeezed into a theoretical straitjacket, cannot stand up to this rebellious, anarchic thrust. Its role turns out, in general, to be a lot more ambiguous, at the point of contact between denunciation and glorification.

The education programs of young curators have to react to this evolution—in a time where the prepossessing dominance of strictly artistic categories has faded out in favor of more general values deriving from human sciences and anthropology. One major subject for the education of independent curators should be anthropology. My suggestion in terms of human sciences would be to teach them anthropology in a way that allows them to use it in a more active way than just quoting the anthropological and philosophical theories of Claude Levy-Strauss, Marc Augé, James Clifford, Jean Baudrillard or Michel Foucault in their papers. In using cliché references, art critics simply pay homage to the "fathers" instead of really dealing with the meaning and interrelations with the works. Of course the knowledge of the history of art is a main condition for a solid background of an independent curator, but it should be taught in a completely different way. Not as a system of eternal values and certainties but as a continuous and dynamic flow of permanently changing relationships to the real. The education has to impart the notion of relative values, for example it is essential to know how to make connections between the work of art and its context of space and time.

I do not know so much about the content of individual curatorial training programs. I suspect that in many cases students are taught more about art theory and aesthetical matters than organizing, managing, and fundraising. Again, the knowledge of history of art and art theories is essential and basic for a curatorial career. But one has to see that the job of the classical art historian has evolved very fast. Initially his role was to give a place to the artist in an always evolving chronology. This is not usually a goal for an artist. Nowadays art historians have become simultaneously promoters of young artists, managers, and interpreters. Not to mention their participation in scenography and installations, which means that a creative aspect to the profession has rapidly come into place.

In our time it has certainly become increasingly important for independent curators to know many secondary skills about the art market and its business. Today curators are needed who not only have a good feeling for art but who are able to establish a trustful relationship with the artists. They must know how to help them technically not only to realize and incarnate their ideas but also to survive in the games of the art world. This evolution is quite recent. It did not exist when I started my career. I was always associated with an art institution, even though I organized many exhibitions outside its frame. My knowledge is "external," which I received from discussions and exchanges with independent curators. My understanding is that independent curatorship is really a specific job where one has to "sell" his ideas to institutions or sponsors. The number of ambitious independent curators has risen over the last several years. Due to the multiple points of views and conceptions on contemporary art and due to the lack of sufficient staff the museum is often not able to curate every planned exhibition appropriately. That is why an increasing number of museums demand experts in a specific field and ask for independent curators. It is more efficient for a museum which plans an exhibition with a specific theme to ask a freelance curator who is already specialized in this topic than to require a staff-curator to get acquainted with it. Though there is an increasing demand on independent curators, the rising amount of independent curators leads to an intense and often even fierce competition that results to low wages.

The success of the work of an independent curator depends on the "good will" of institutions and sponsors. Imagining and supporting art events outside institutions suggest at the first glance freedom of action in planning an exhibition but no material and technical support. The infrastructure, the know-how and technical support of a museum often makes the realization of a project a lot easier. Most radical events may happen within institutions where the director can from time to time insert a very risky intervention in his program. This is sometimes easier than convincing a sponsor to produce a totally radical event in art. In this case the sponsor itself must have already been convinced about the trends of contemporary art and must be familiar to the contemporary art world. The independent curator should not be afraid of radicalism which might be inherent to a work of art. On the contrary he has to be open for any discussion that might come up if he sponsors a social or political critical work of art.

The scene of contemporary art is full of conflicts of interests, especially since museums have become interested in young artists and endorsing them. In Europe this phenomena is not that new as one might expect. Many museums of the 19th century were collecting living art, i.e., contemporary art of their time, to support local or local born artists. With the rise of modernism in the end of the 19th century the interest and understanding of the museum for contemporary art was interrupted for at most one century. In France especially museums did not risk purchasing modern art for a long time. This attitude was even supported by collectors or art dealers, who themselves championed burgeoning artists. They believed in the theory of Kahnweiler who claimed that only the art market, which meant exclusively collectors and gallerists, had to deal with living art and not public institutions. In his opinion museums should only purchase works of artists that had proven that their works had still an intellectual and financial value for the following generations of collectors, who judge works with the distance of time. He believed in a "filter effect" of time. Works of living art are mostly supported by collectors, who are more or less the same age as the artists. It is after the disappearance of this generation that important falls or rises in value occur.

This raises the question: Is the museum supposed to be an institution to establish aesthetical and artistic value compared to the market value or rather should it be a place for the promotion of new coming artists? Obviously doing both at the same time is a difficult challenge. Promoting new artists on the one hand and keeping an historical critical point of view on the other hand is not very easy, but I have always tried to go for such a challenge. To be successful an independent curator needs a good critical approach to tastes and trends in art, a good critical background. Therefore my proposal for the curatorial program would be to draw the attention of students to the incredibly fast change of taste and trends, in other words to the fashion in art through the 20th century. The students should deal with questions like: What was highlighted at each period? What was purchased by different museums at the same time? One should also study the evolution of the collections of the big museums of modern art in the last century: When were the masterpieces of today purchased? What were the masterpieces fifty or eighty years ago? Which works were shown in the galleries and which ones hidden in storage at different periods of time? Students have to understand history of art as a continuous and dynamic flowing process of realities.

But even if the museums now are much more open to new trends in contemporary art than in the 19th century, it still seems to be very difficult to combine the work of independent curators with the code of ethics edicted by ICOM, i.e., the curator cannot be active as a private collector in the field of his competence in the museum.

Through lack of courage or taste for risk, many museums have not yet taken the measure of the freedom they are being offered. Most of the criticism directed at my exhibition *Magiciens de la Terre* resulted from this audacious demonstration of the degree to which the art world, which saw itself as being so free, or even libertarian, had been building up geographical boundaries. The bigger the museum, the more it is closed up within its limits and contradictions.

Promoting artists independently is very close to marketing and selling art. There are independent curators who receive works from the artists in exchange for their help or services. This was a common practice with critics until the 60s. The power switched from the critics to the independent curators in the 70s. Writing about works of art, interpreting them, gives them an intellectual, ideological, and spiritual value. This can be conveyed through written explanations although the display of the works in a show can help a lot for its understanding. It is usually what the art dealer is not able to deliver and where he needs academic support. In the 60s artists were looking for famous critics whose names were a "guarantee." Since the 70s they have been more interested in the support of well-known curators and in their inclusion in certain exhibitions.

Advising collections is a difficult field, too. The work for an independent curator in this field depends on the attitude of the collector. If the collector is deeply involved in arts and knows about the movements he is interested in he might only need some assistance, an expert who has a broader specific knowledge and who is able to put the works of art in a special context that the collector may not have considered. The independent curator has the role of a "scout," who is looking for pieces of art according to the collector's line. If the collector directs his attention to "successful" and already well-known artists, the independent curator has to seek artists who have the most chances to get a quick added value in the art market. For this part the independent curator also needs good connections to art dealers. He has to build up a trustful relationship in order to get the "right" pieces in time. The independent curator has to be part of the game of the art market, which makes it very difficult for him to hold the distance that allows him a considered and long-run foreseeing judgement.

The independent curator is the link between the creator and the public. To make access for the public possible, he needs to set up the right conditions to realize artistic projects. That means he has to find the right institution to show the artist's work and he has to clear the financial situation. If the artist does not make a visual object, for instance if he creates purely conceptual works of art, it is the job of an independent curator to deliver all possible comments and interpretations to help the public understand the work and to get a feeling for it.

The independent curator should discuss the project with the artist to avoid a sort of utopian project, whose realization stays half way from its goal and leads to disappointment, or hermetic works without a consistent theory in the background. Young artists often have a big fantasy about their ideas, what their works are supposed to convey, and about the possible imagined reception by the public. They always credit the viewer with much more than his normal capacity. It is the task of the independent curator to make them aware of which sensations their work might communicate and the best display of the elements in an exhibition so the idea of the work is supported at its best. Conversations with artists require diplomacy because some artists may refuse any interference in their artistic decisions, so that there may be no flexibility and room for discussion. Others might be more open to a discussion. Of course these two attitudes do not take into account the talent and the quality of the artist.

A big change in curatorship happened throughout the 60s and 70s. Curators started to withdraw from institutional rules governing the format of the work of art and began to concentrate on the integrity of an artist's project in the artistic program of the museum, even if it might challenge the institution's programmatic direction—although not in the same intense way that again today the question is regularly raised. But it is important to make a clear distinction between utopian projects that have to be shown as such with possible realization in the future (when the needed technology is currently not available or too expensive) and feasible projects. Artists have to be warned sometimes of too exaggerated excesses of free imagination. If the project is not feasible as conceived, it is again the task of the independent curator to find together with the artist a way to realize it. This process needs elevated sensitivity because there is nothing worse in an exhibition than uncompleted projects, when the idea of a work of art had to be changed from the original idea just because the required technology was not available to the artist. A work of art should only be shown after the independent curator and the artist have explored all possible ways to realize it. Not only the technical, but also the political, and financial conditions have to be cleared and applied to the realization of the project. These comments are not only relevant for the independent curator but also for curators who are working for an institution. An important turning point in this direction was the exhibition by Harald Szeemann *Live In Your Head: When Attitudes Become Form* in Bern 1969. Artists were allocated a more or less open space and they made the show. The role of the curator was to help to realize the project with his full support.

One of the most important roles of an independent curator is to help unknown artists get settled in the art scene in finding the right places and conditions to make the display of the work possible. In this case finding money outside existing institutions is always very difficult. Convincing possible sponsors to contribute is among the best qualities an independent curator has to possess. Again, diplomatic skills and passion are needed.

A talent in communication is also one of the main requirements for good independent curatorship. The independent curator must be able to deal with all possible media of communication. To convince the specialized media of the excellence of an artist.he is endorsing might be one of his hardest jobs. Again this is a risky field. The interpretation and explanation he may give of the work are essential for the diffusion of the ideas conveyed by the work not only for art lovers but also for a larger public. He must find a balance between the intentions and statements of the artists and his own ideas and interpretation that might differ.

Whether these explanations of the work should be available in a written or oral form lies by the artist in agreement with the independent curator. Some artists may refuse any pedagogical material next to their work—a highly respectable decision. In this case it is the work of an independent curator to display the work of art in the exhibition in a way that provokes the most efficient sensations from it. The independent curator must use the instrument of "visual pedagogy" instead of "discursive pedagogy."

Curators sometimes spend a dreadful lot of time explaining what art is and why this or that new work, which does not correspond to the traditional canon of art, or should actually be considered as such. It is astonishing that they do not devote more time to understanding why so many items of today's material culture are not recognized as art. In every field of knowledge evolution results from self-criticism and from questioning not only the paradigms of the discipline but also the boundaries set by the taxonomy. The necessity of defining an autonomy of art has led to an endogamy of the relation system in art.

Curators should not only concentrate on the culture of our times and radius, i.e., western culture, but also on the culture of non-western societies. I see an essential duty of curatorial work in discovering the diversity of aesthetic expressions of, in our eyes, exotic cultures. Globalization forces the opening up of the closed circle of western contemporary art. This has partially been done during the last fifteen years by including artists coming from other countries in international exhibitions, for example in the Havana Biennales since 1986 or in the exhibition *Africa Explores: 20th century African Art* at the New Museum of Contemporary Art, New York in 1991. These artists may be seen as an alibi, because in most cases they belong to the post-modern movement and they are plugged into the usual western art network. A real understanding of and a dialogue with other cultures can only be achieved through a fundamental questioning of the history of art the way it has been written by the west. The hierarchy of values of techniques and artistic practices must be questioned. It has always been the system of values of western culture, which for us has decided between art and craft, between major and minor genres, between authentic and folkloristic. The scale of values needs to be reevaluated in a post-colonial perspective. But there are many obstacles that prevent seeing the western art system in relative terms and rewriting the history of art.

The European culpability towards colonialism leads to a fear of everything different coming from a foreign culture, in the name of preventing exoticism, always seen only in its negative side, i.e., the instrumentalization of the other for the exclusive superficial pleasure of a few rich amateurs. The number of clichés conveyed in this regard is considerable. The way exoticism is criticized corresponds to television: we are all TV consumers and tourists, it all depends what we make of it.

Another major barrier is our inability to see western culture in relative terms, especially in modernism. As long as the Hegelian theory, which is the basis of modernist and post theory, rules the understanding of art and is projected—in a very neo-colonial way—on foreign cultures, there will be no chance to establish a real dialogue with them. Equality could be more easily sought for cultures than for politics or economy. A geo-cultural approach shows how inconsistent the art "system" is. Most of the artworks of the past displayed in museums belong to religion, magic, and funeral rites. Why is it that because of colonialist exploitation, projection of modernism on others and diffusion of Christianity, authentic artistic value is denied to any visual expression of religion today? Given this absurd paradox, visual art is in this regard the most reactionary discipline in western culture.

This narrow minded thinking forgets that first of all it should be the presence of the work of art that conveys a sensation for its aesthetical value. The definition of the term of "exoticism" depends on the perspective of perception. So the notion of "exoticism" can be extended to the western hemisphere and reverse the usual viewpoint: the western view is no longer focused on, but it is complimented by, the perspective held by non-western cultures on the occidental world.

Artists and museums have for too long taken advantage of the geographical or intellectual remoteness of certain formal types of expression. Many intellectuals who would consider themselves to be above any accusation of racism are far from accepting the idea of equality among different artistic values. The art market prefers artists who are familiar with the methods and strategies of the western art market, it has no interest for exotic cultures, except for the countries that promise an economic upturn, like China or Russia. How many curators are travelling to Africa to discover living artists on-site? Not to mention art dealers.

Passion, curiosity, and honesty must always be the main interests of a curator who wants to convey his enthusiasm to other people. A curator should try to interpret our world and to understand it in its whole diversity. Therefore independent thinking—independent curatorship—is required.

Now based in Paris, museum director and exhibition organizer Jean-Hubert Martin served as General Director of the museum kunst palast in Düsseldorf from 2000-2006. He has received great esteem and recognition internationally, in particular with the *Magiciens de la Terre* exhibition in 1989 and the way he had drawn together exhibits from all over the world and for the first time presented non-western art on equal terms, and also for his work on the biennales at Lyon (2000), São Paulo (1996), Johannesburg (1995), and Sydney (1993 and 1982), and as a conceiver and host of other remarkable exhibitions. His previous positions include Curator at the Musée National d'art Moderne, Paris; Director, Kunsthalle, Bern; Director, Musée National d'Art Moderne, Centre Georges Pompidou, Paris; Artistic Director, Château d'Oiron; and Director, Musée National des Arts d'Afrique et d'Océanie, Paris.

Boris Groys

The Curator as Iconoclast

The work of the curator consists of placing artworks in the exhibition space. This is what differentiates the curator from the artist, as the artist has the privilege to exhibit objects that have not already been elevated to the status of artworks. In fact, they gain this status precisely through their placement in the exhibition space. Duchamp exhibiting a urinal is not a curator but an artist, because his decision to present the urinal in the framework of an exhibition has made this urinal a work of art. This opportunity is denied to the curator. He can of course exhibit a urinal, but only if it is Duchamp's urinal—that is, a urinal that has already obtained its art status. The curator can easily exhibit an unsigned urinal, one without art status, but it will merely be regarded as an example of a certain period of European design, serve as "contextualization" for exhibited artworks, or fulfill some other subordinate function. In no way can this urinal obtain art status—and after the end of the exhibition it will return not to the museum, but back where it came from. The curator may exhibit, but he doesn't have the magical ability to transform non-art into art through the act of display. That power, according to current cultural conventions, belongs to the artist alone.

It hasn't been always so. Originally art became art through the decisions of curators, rather than artists. The first art museums came into existence at the turn of the 19th century and became established in the course of that century as a consequence of revolutions, wars, imperial conquest, and pillage of non-European cultures. All kinds of "beautiful" functional objects, previously employed for various religious rituals, dressing the rooms of power, or manifesting private wealth, were collected and put on display as works of art—that is, as defunctionalized, autonomous objects of pure contemplation. The curators administering these museums "created" art through iconoclastic acts directed against traditional icons of religion or power, by reducing these icons to mere artworks. Art was originally "just" art. This perception of it as such is situated within the tradition of the European Enlightenment, which conceived of all religious icons as "simple things"—and art solely as beautiful objects, as mere artworks. The question then is: Why have curators lost the power to create art through the act of its exhibition, and why has this power passed to artists?

The answer is obvious: In exhibiting a urinal, Duchamp does not devalue a sacred icon, as the museum curators did; he rather upgrades a mass-produced object to an artwork. In this way the exhibition's role in the symbolic economy changes. Sacred objects were once devalued to produce art; today, in contrast, profane objects are valorized to become art. What was originally iconoclasm has turned into iconophilia. But this shift in the symbolic economy had already been put in motion by the curators and art critics of the 19th century.

Every exhibition tells a story, by directing the viewer through itself in a particular order; the exhibition space is always a narrative space. The traditional art museum told the story of art's emergence and subsequent victory. Individual artworks chronicled this story—and in doing so lost their old religious or representative significance and gained new meaning. Once museums had emerged as the new place of worship, artists began to work specifically for the museum. Historically significant objects no longer needed to be devalued in order to serve as art. Instead, brand new, profane objects became recognized as artworks because they allegedly embodied the new artistic value. These objects didn't have a prehistory, nor had they been legitimized by religion or power. At most they could be regarded as signs of a "simple, everyday life" with indeterminate value. Their inscription into art history meant valorization for these objects, not devaluation. Museums had been transformed from places of Enlightenment-inspired iconoclasm into places of romantic iconophilia. Exhibiting an object as art no longer signified its profanation, but its sacralization. Duchamp simply took this change to its final conclusion when he laid bare the iconophilic mechanism of valorization of mere things by labeling them works of art.

Over the years modern artists began to assert their art's total autonomy—and not just from its sacred prehistory, but from art history as well: Every integration of an image into a story, every appropriation of it as illustration for a particular narrative, is iconoclastic—even if the story is that of a triumph of this image, its transfiguration or its glorification. According to the tradition of modern art, an image must speak for itself; it must immediately convince the spectator, standing in silent contemplation, of its own value. The conditions in which the work is exhibited should be reduced to white walls and good lighting. Theoretical and narrative babble must stop. Even affirmative discourse and a favorable display are regarded as distorting the message of the artwork itself. So modern artists began to hate and condemn curators, because the curators never could completely rid themselves of their iconoclastic heritage. They couldn't but place, contextualize, and narrativize works of art—which necessarily led to the relativization of those works of art. Curating's ineradicable and inevitable iconoclasm has never made artists happy; museums have been compared to graveyards, and curators to undertakers. With such insults (disguised as institutional critique), artists won the general public over to their side, because the general public didn't know all the history; it didn't even want to hear it. The public wishes to be confronted directly with individual artworks and exposed to their unmediated impact. It steadfastly believes in the autonomous meaning of the individual artwork, which is supposedly being manifested in front of its eyes. The curator's every mediation is suspect: he is seen as someone standing between the artwork and its viewer, insidiously manipulating the viewer's perception with the intent of disempowering the public. That's why, for the general public, the art market is more enjoyable than any museum. Artworks circulating on the market are singled out, decontextualized, uncurated—so they get the apparently unadulterated chance to demonstrate their inherent value. Consequently the art market is an extreme example of what Marx termed commodity fetishism, meaning a belief in the inherent value of an object, its value being its intrinsic quality. Thus began a time of degradation and distress for curators—the time of modern art. Curators have managed their degradation surprisingly well, though, by successfully internalizing it.

Even today we hear from many curators that they are working toward a single objective: making individual artworks appear in the most favorable light. Or, to put it differently, that the best curating is nil-curating, noncurating. From this perspective, the solution seems to be to let the artwork alone, enabling the viewer to confront it directly. However, not even the renowned white cube is always good enough for this purpose. The viewer is often advised to completely abstract himself from the work's spatial surroundings, and to immerse himself fully in self- and world-denying contemplation. Under these conditions alone—beyond any kind of curating, that is—can the encounter with an artwork be regarded as authentic and genuinely successful. That such contemplation cannot go ahead without the artwork's being exhibited, however, remains an indisputable fact. Giorgio Agamben writes that "the image is a being, that in its essence is appearance, visibility, or semblance."[1] But this definition of artwork's essence does not suffice to guarantee the visibility of a concrete artwork. A work of art can't in fact present itself by virtue of its own definition and force the viewer into contemplation—artworks lack vitality, energy, and health. They seem to be genuinely sick and helpless; a spectator has to be led to the artwork, as hospital workers might take a visitor to see a bedridden patient. It is no coincidence that the word "curator" is etymologically related to "cure." Curating is curing. The process of curating cures the image's powerlessness, its incapacity to present itself. The artwork needs external help; it needs an exhibition and a curator to become visible. The medicine that makes the sick image appear healthy—makes the image literally appear, and in the best light—is the exhibition. In this respect, since iconophilia is dependent upon the image appearing healthy and strong, the curatorial practice is, to a certain degree, the servant of iconophilia.

But at the same time, curatorial practice undermines iconophilia, for its medical artifice cannot remain entirely concealed from the viewer. In this respect, curating remains unintentionally iconoclastic even as it is programmatically iconophilic. Indeed, curating acts as a supplement or a pharmacon (in Derrida's usage[2]), in that it cures the image even as it makes it unwell. Curating cannot escape being simultaneously iconophilic and iconoclastic. Yet this opens the question: Which is the right kind of curatorial practice? Since curatorial practice can never totally conceal itself, the main objective of curating must be to visualize itself, by making its practice explicitly visible. The will for visualization is in fact what constitutes and drives art. Since it takes place within the context of art, curatorial practice cannot elude the logic of visibility.

The visualization of curating demands a simultaneous mobilization of its iconoclastic potential. Of course, contemporary iconoclasm can and should be aimed primarily not at religious icons but at art itself. By placing an artwork in a controlled environment; in the context of other carefully chosen objects; and above all in the framework of a specific story, a narrative, the curator is making an iconoclastic gesture. If this gesture is made explicit enough, curating returns to its secular beginnings, withstanding the transformation of art into art-as-religion, and becomes an expression of art-atheism. The fetishization of art is taking place outside the museum, meaning outside the zone in which the curator has traditionally exercised authority. These days, artworks become iconic not as a result of their display in the museum but of their circulation in the art market and in mass media. Under these circumstances, the curating of an artwork signifies its return to history, the transformation of the autonomous artwork back into an illustration, an illustration whose value is not contained within itself but is extrinsic, attached to an historical narrative.

Orhan Pamuk's novel *My Name is Red* features a group of artists searching for a place for art within an iconoclastic culture, namely that of 16th century Islamic Turkey. The group is comprised of illustrators commissioned by the powerful to ornament their books with exquisite miniatures; subsequently, these books are placed in governmental or private collections. Not only are these artists increasingly being persecuted by radical Islamic (iconoclastic) adversaries who want to ban all images, they are also in competition with the occidental painters of the Renaissance, primarily Venetians, who openly affirm their own iconophilia. Yet the novel's heroes can't share this iconophilia, because they don't believe in the autonomy of images. And so they try to find a way to take a consistently honest iconoclastic stance without abandoning the terrain of art. A Turkish sultan, whose theory of art would actually serve as good advice for contemporary curatorial practice, shows them the way.

The sultan says the following: "An illustration that does not complement a story, in the end, will become but a false idol. Since we cannot possibly believe in the absent story, we will naturally begin believing in the picture itself. This would be no different than the worship of the idols in the Kaaba that went on before Our Prophet, peace and blessings be upon him, had destroyed them.... If I believed, heaven forbid, the way these infidels do, that the Prophet Jesus was also the Lord God himself ... only then might I accept the depiction of mankind in full detail and exhibit such images. You do understand that, eventually, we would then unthinkingly begin worshipping any picture that is hung on the wall, don't you?"[3]

Strong iconoclastic tendencies and currents were naturally to be found in the Christian Occident as well—in 20th century modern art in particular; indeed, most modern art was created through iconoclasm. As a matter of fact, the avant-garde staged a martyrdom of the image, which replaced the Christian image of martyrdom. It put traditional painting through all sorts of tortures, which recall first and foremost the tortures to which the saints were subjected as depicted in paintings from the Middle Ages. Thus the image is—symbolically and literally—sawed, cut, fragmented, drilled, pierced, dragged through the dirt, and left to the mercy of ridicule. No coincidence, then, that the historical avant-garde consistently employed the language of iconoclasm: avant-garde artists speak of demolishing traditions, breaking with conventions, destroying their artistic heritage, and annihilating old values. But this is definitely not a matter of sadistic lust for the abuse of innocent images, nor is there any guarantee that new images or new values will emerge as a consequence of all this demolition and annihilation. Quite the contrary: images of demolition of old icons become new icons for the new values. The iconoclastic gesture is instituted here as an artistic method, less for the annihilation of old icons than for the production of new images—or, if you want, new icons and new idols.

Actually, the iconoclastic gesture, if understood as the act of destruction of old idols, was never a manifestation of an atheist or skeptical position. The destruction of old idols only takes place in the name of other, newer gods. Specifically, iconoclasm wants to prove that the old gods have become powerless and can no longer protect their earthly temples and images. Thus the iconoclast takes religion's claim to power seriously, in that his destructive actions disprove the power of the old gods in order to affirm the power of his own. Traditional iconoclasm functions as a mechanism for the reevaluation of values, destroying old values and idols in order to institute new ones. Christianity appropriated and neutralized this traditional iconoclastic gesture, because in the Christian tradition the image of destruction and destitution—Christ on the cross—is transformed quasi-automatically into an image of the triumph of that which has been destroyed. Our iconographic imagination, which has long been honed by the Christian tradition, does not hesitate to recognize victory in the image of defeat. In fact, here the defeat is a victory from the start. Modern art has benefited significantly from the adoption of iconoclasm as a mode of production.

Indeed, throughout the era of Modernism, every time an iconoclastic image has been produced, hung on the wall, or presented in an exhibition space, it has become an idol. The reason is clear: modern art has struggled particularly hard against the image's illustrative use and its narrative function. The result of this struggle illustrates the sultan's premonition. Modern art wanted to purify the image of everything exterior to it, to render the image autonomous and self-sufficient, but in so doing it only affirmed the dominant iconophilia. Iconoclasm has become subordinate to iconophilia: the image's symbolic martyrdom only strengthens belief in it.

The subtler iconoclastic strategy proposed by the sultan—turning the image back into an illustration—is in fact much more effective. We have known at least since Magritte that when we look at an image of a pipe, we are not regarding a real pipe but one that has been painted. The pipe as such isn't there, isn't present; instead, it is being depicted as absent. In spite of this knowledge, we are still inclined to believe that when we look at an artwork, we directly and instantaneously confront "art." We see artworks as incarnating art. The famous distinction between art and non-art is generally understood as a distinction between objects inhabited and animated by art, and those from which art is absent. This is how works of art become art's idols—that is, analogous to religious images, which are also believed to be inhabited or animated by gods.

On the other hand, to practice art-atheism would mean understanding artworks not as incarnations, but as mere documents, illustrations, or signifiers of art. While they may refer to art, these are nevertheless not the genuine article. To a greater or lesser extent, this strategy has been pursued by many artists since the 1960s. Artistic projects, performances, and actions have regularly been documented, and by means of this documentation represented in exhibition spaces and museums. However, such documentation simply refers to art without itself being art. This type of documentation is often presented in the framework of an art installation for the purpose of narrating a certain project or action. Traditionally executed paintings, art objects, photographs, and videos can also be utilized in the framework of such installations. In this case, admittedly, artworks lose their usual status as art. Instead they become documents, illustrations of the story told by the installation. One could say that today's art audience increasingly encounters art *documentation*, which provides information about the artwork itself, be it art project or art action, but in doing so confirms the absence of the artwork.

But even if "illustrativity" and "narrativity" have managed to find their way into the halls of art, by no means does this entry signify the automatic triumph of art-atheism. Even if the artist becomes faithless, he or she doesn't lose the magical ability to transform the simplest thing into art, just as a Catholic priest's loss of faith doesn't render the rituals he performs ineffective. Meanwhile, the installation itself has been blessed with art status: it has become accepted as an art form and increasingly assumes a leading role in contemporary art. Though the individual images and objects lose their autonomous status, the entire installation gains it back. When Marcel Broodthaers presented his *Musée d'Art Moderne, Département des Aigles* at the Kunsthalle in Dusseldorf in 1973, he placed the label "This is not a work of art" next to each of the presented objects in the installation. The installation as a whole, though, is legitimately considered to be an artwork.

Here the figure of the independent curator, increasingly central to contemporary art, comes into play. When it comes down to it, the independent curator is doing everything the contemporary artist does. The independent curator travels the world and organizes exhibitions that are comparable to artistic installations, because they are the results of individual curatorial projects, decisions, and actions. Artworks presented in these exhibitions/installations take on the role of documentation of a curatorial project. Yet such curatorial projects are in no way iconophilic; they don't aim to glorify art's autonomous value.

Utopia Station is a good example. Curated by Molly Nesbit, Hans Ulrich Obrist, and Rirkrit Tiravanija, this exhibition was presented at the 50th Venice Biennale in 2003. Critical and public discussion of it focused on whether the concept of utopia is still relevant in this day and age, whether what was being put forward as a utopian vision by the curators could really be regarded as such, and so on. Yet the fact that a curatorial project that was clearly iconoclastic could be presented at one of the oldest international art exhibitions seems to me far more important than the above considerations. *Utopia Station* was iconoclastic because it employed artworks as illustrations, as documents of the search for a social utopia, without emphasizing their autonomous value. It subscribed to the radical, iconoclastic approach of the Russian avant-garde, which considered art to be documentation of the search for the "new man" and a "new life." Most important, though, *Utopia Station* was a curatorial and not an artistic project (even if one the curators, Tiravanija, is an artist). This meant that the iconoclastic gesture could not be accompanied—and thus invalidated—by the attribution of artistic value. Nevertheless, it can still be assumed that even in this case the concept of utopia was abused, because it was aestheticized and situated in an elitist art context. And it can be equally said that art was abused as well: it served as an illustration for the curator's vision of utopia. In both cases, the spectator has to confront an abuse, be it through art or by art. Here, though, abuse is just another word for iconoclasm.

The independent curator is a radically secularized artist. He is an artist because he does everything artists do. But the independent curator is an artist who has lost the artist's aura, one who no longer has magical powers at his disposal, who cannot endow objects with art's status. He doesn't use objects—art objects included—for art's sake, but rather abuses them, makes them profane. Yet it is precisely this practice that makes the figure of the independent curator so attractive and so essential to the art of today. The contemporary curator is heir apparent to the modern artist, although he doesn't suffer under his predecessor's magical abnormalities. He is an artist, but also atheistic and "normal" through and through. The curator is an agent of art's profanation, its secularization, its profane abuse. It can of course be stated that the independent curator, like the museum curator before him, cannot but depend on the art market—even do the groundwork for it. An artwork's value increases when it is presented in a museum or through its frequent appearance in the diverse temporary exhibitions organized by independent curators, and so, as before, the dominant iconophilia prevails. This can be held to be self-evident—or not.

The market value of an artwork doesn't correspond exactly to its narrative or its historical value. The traditional "museum value" of an artwork is never the same as its value on the art market. A work of art can please, impress, excite the desire to possess it—all this while not having a specific historical relevance, and therefore remaining irrelevant to the museum's narrative. And, turning this around, many artworks that may seem incomprehensible, boring, and depressing to the general public find their place in the museum, because they are "historically new" or at the very least "relevant" to a particular period, and therefore can be put to the task of illustrating a certain kind of art history. The widespread opinion that an artwork in a museum is "dead" can be understood as meaning that it loses its status as an idol there; pagan idols were venerated for being "alive." The museum's iconoclastic gesture consists precisely of the transformation of "living" idols into "dead" illustrations for art history. It can therefore be said that the traditional museum curator has always subjected images to the same double abuse as the independent curator has. On one hand, images in the museum are aestheticized and transformed into art; on the other, they are downgraded to illustrations of art history and thereby dispossessed of their art status.

This double abuse of images, this doubled iconoclastic gesture, is only recently being made explicit, because instead of narrating the canon of art history, independent curators are beginning to tell each other their own contradictory stories. In addition, these stories are being told by means of temporary exhibitions (which carry their own time limitations) and recorded by incomplete and frequently even incomprehensible documentation. The exhibition catalog for a curatorial project that already presents a double abuse can only produce a further abuse. But nevertheless, artworks become visible only as a result of this multiple abuse. Images don't emerge into the clearing of Being on their own accord, in order for their original visibility to be muddied by the "art business," as Heidegger describes it in *The Origin of the Work of Art*. It is far more that this very abuse is what makes them visible.

1. Giorgio Agamben, *Propfanierungen* (Frankfurt: Suhrkamp, 2005), p. 53.
2. Jacques Derrida, *La dissemination* (Paris: Editions du Seuil, 1972), pp. 108f.
3. Orhan Pamuk, *My Name Is Red* (New York: Alfred Knopf, 2001), pp. 109-110.

Translated by Elena Sorokina.

Boris Groys, Professor of Philosophy and Art Theory at the Academy for Design in Karlsruhe, Germany, and Global Professor at New York University, is one of the greatest experts and theoretical scholars in the reflection of modern art. Member of the Association International des Critiques d'Art (AICA) since 1991. He has written and edited numerous books, including *Dnevnik filosofa* (russ.) [*Diary of a Philosopher*] (Paris, 1989); *Gesamtkunstwerk Stalin* (Munich, 1988); *Die Kunst der Installation* [with Ilya Kabakov] (Munich, 1996); and *Unter Verdacht. Eine Phänomenologie der Medien* (Munich, 2000). Groys organized *The Art Judgment Show*, a televised talk show on the state of art, in 2001.

Geeta Kapur

Curating: In the Public Sphere

In the Wake of the 1960s: Curators and Avant-garde Practice

A curated show may render an individual artwork less "itself," less than it is in the studio or within the more dedicated aesthetic framework of a monographic show or in the discreet display of an art-historical museum. More controversially, the curator may deliberately render the artwork incomplete and construct (deconstruct) meanings with reference to a conceptual paradigm, or, on the other hand, a spectatorial schema in which it is seen as only an instance. In this case, the curator can be said to be acting against the interest of the artist in order to act in favor of some new relational premise between works and with the beholders. I favor looking at an exhibition as an *itinerary*, and an *argument*, where the curatorially determined itinerary and the expositional argument are intertwined and unfold in time to a walking rhythm, and where the installed exhibition, a synchronous structure supported by a *mise-en-scène*, is staged by the curator.

The role of the curator as the creative director of an exhibition emerged in the late 60s.[1] It developed rapidly by incorporating the artistic and intellectual preoccupations of the time. A glance at some examples of the 60s art movements shows how changed art forms demand a corresponding style of exposition within the gallery, how curatorial innovations occur with reference to structures, models, ideologies devised for specific tendencies. Minimalism, for example, suggested that the spectatorial body has an axial privilege, that it provides a phenomenological understanding of the artwork. Translated into curatorial practice, it required an astute positioning of the artwork in the spatial discourse of the exhibition, and it required that the curator find ways to restrain the exhibition process at the very point where the controlled theater of the encounter turns into spectacle.

The 60s critique of the consumer society in late capitalism—what Guy Debord called the "society of the spectacle"—translated into a renewed understanding of historical materialism and triggered a response in the discourse on art whereby the growing reification of the art object was put under scrutiny. Arte Povera offered new forms of material investment in objects that were then outside of the exchange nexus and signaled subversive messages in favor of inversion and redundancy. The Fluxus movement swooped across standard taxonomies and value hierarchies in art, upturning exhibition procedures right down to the scale, devices and containers for display. At the same time, "happenings" (already preceded by the action-oriented art of the Gutai artists in 50s Japan) erupted in the art scene, privileging improvisation and transience, followed in the 70s by a more structured performance art led by feminists.

The 60s breakthrough was crucial in reintroducing radical forms of material and symbolic *entropy* into art; in consequence, exhibition-making canons were destabilized, and democratic initiatives put pressure on the very institution of art. The landmark exhibition of that period, by the "master" curator, Harald Szeemann, took place in 1969. It was tellingly called *Live in Your Head: When Attitude Become Form: Works-Concepts-Processes-Situations-Information.*[2] Szeemann favored flux, ferment, and a process-oriented sociability rather than an object fixation in the making and showing of artworks, and he emphasized a radical individualism ("inner bearing") and a utopian romance by and on behalf of the artist. He set the stage for the curator as collaborator and co-producer of artworks and exhibitions alike, and he would be for decades to come an avant-garde figure in his own right.

The following decades saw the rise of architectural-scale installations, site-specific projects, interactive community workshops, and an anarchic spillage into social spaces by artists and curators working to build an alternative infrastructure to the gallery system.[3] The idea of the art laboratory was afloat, and the ideological issue of art in the public domain became prominent in the discourse.

The democratic impulse also took another route precisely in the late 60s,[4] extending the emerging practice of Conceptualism through a corresponding curatorial reflexivity. Conceptual art, intent on unmaking the art object, privileged intellectual economy and an almost unprecedented form of austerity regarding the means and ends of art. The white cube was emptied out and made neutral, even at times redundant for and by Conceptual art. This discreet, deliberately anti-experiential space served two paradoxical ends: to permit access to texts (documentation) in a commonplace way; and to instill the philosophic indeterminacy of esoteric messages and everyday conundrums in clinical conditions. This double encounter was designated as "art" that has finally done away with its aura.

The developments sketched briefly above are condensed in my example of Catherine David's *DocumentaX* at Kassel (1997). David created a new discursive space for cuaratorship in which the collaborative model was reshaped by a form of curatorial command—for example, in the way she laid out what she called the *parcours*, the itinerary, and through it an argument for the exposition, using the city as the *mise-en-scène*. A selection of key avant-garde moves from the 60s to the present was restaged to testify for what she saw as *critical* art practice with a corresponding poetics and a related, politically inspired discourse.[5] David's range of choices first defined her position within the contemporary; then, deploying the privilege of curatorial detachment, she "exceeded" the artists' intent. Arching over the actual artworks on display was something like a problematic, a metadiscourse on what critical contemporaneity in art might mean today. This made the exhibition a philosophic case in point, an exegesis as much as a phenomenological experience—and the "Hundred Days Hundred Guests" program of lectures, which drew in multidisciplinary and worldwide extrapolation on contemporary forms of criticality, was part of that exegesis.

The 1980s: Curating in a Heterogeneous World

Here, now, I step outside the Euroamerican zone and into the world where curatorial practices have developed contingent, even indeed exigent, styles, often in contrast to those sanctioned by (western) art history. The rise of the curator as a key category in the exposition of art happens, coincidentally, in tandem with the third-world assertions of alterity, including a revolutionary passage in the 60s and a more conciliatory form of multiculturalism since. Standard discourse on contemporary art, destabilized by the onset of post-colonial post-modernism, was relativized for good in the 80s. Consequently, the curatorial project today entails an almost mandatory inclusiveness based on *difference*.

Jean-Hubert Martin's controversial exhibition *Magiciens de la Terre* at the Centre Georges Pompidou (Paris, 1989)[6] serves as a trigger for this part of the argument, situating Europe's perennial interest in the exotic within the new transculturist permissiveness of the postmodern. In *Magiciens*, Martin gave something like a ritual status to contemporary avant-garde art of the west, relating this to the allegedly magic-driven artworks from "other" cultures. Correspondingly, he contemporized the "sacred" works from the margins in conjunction with the declaredly secular works from the west. This relativizing exercise, meant to revise the debate about the "primitive" and the modern, was also intended, presumably, to produce a conviviality between races and genres.

Magiciens was based on an (ethnographic) anachronism, a categorization in which the diachronic tension between primitive and modern, traditional and avant-garde—an important tension—was fudged by the generous aesthetic and supposed equation of synchronous viewing, only to resurface as other (objectionable) criteria. My criticism is that the paradigm for contemporary art was based on the binary of the *indigenous* and the *avant-garde*, on seeing these categories (yet again) in geographical terms: the avant-garde mapped over the northern zone, the indigenous across the south, encouraging further demarcations that maintain the center-periphery model. Weighed as a balance of potentialities, this schema attributes *individual agency* to western artists, *timeless consanguinity* to others. Predictably, therefore, examples of transformative art practices in non-western societies—metropolitan art practices of long standing—were barely included. Few protagonists were located within the highly differentiated societies outside the west and shown to have agency that is properly historical: where a self-conscious breakthrough in language and politics takes place, and where that is seen to make a conceptual contribution to the western claim on the avant-garde.

And yet, I would say, *Magiciens* was a provocation worth its while. Certainly, a part of the credit for the way these ideas have been thrashed out and tested in discourse and in regional exhibitions ever since must go to its bold topography across continents. The important thing is that this argument has been taken to the sites in question—in terms of history *and* geography—where the semiotic grid of signs and meanings can be shown to be embedded in the material conditions of their production. And the politics of the artistic moves that result from this plotting have to be read by the curator diachronically, given that the societies in question recognize their own historicity.

In 1996, the Asia Society in New York mounted an important exhibition titled *Contemporary Art of Asia: Tradition/Tensions*,[7] with a range of artworks prominent among which were installations with an explicit materiality, site-specific and performative interventions and documentary inputs with political annotations. It presented artists with a rich understanding of a situational phenomenology that locates their work and demands a spectatorial comprehension at the cutting edge between ritual protocol and political transgression. The curator, Apinan Poshyananda, presented the exhibition as both contrastive and complementary to western "models." Without being ideologized as such, it had a built-in pedagogy with regard to other types of viewing protocol. For example, it proposed that the sacred, even when placed in parenthesis, sets up a customary etiquette whereby the phenomenology of the exhibition is restructured. Notions of invocation/circumambulation, of intimacy/distance, replace the "detached" encounter of western aesthetics.

This culturally replete aesthetic, this experiential rendering of the esoteric *and* the political privileged by the first phase of Asian art exhibitions, was upturned in *Cities on the Move* (1997-99), a way-out and widely toured exhibition curated by Hou Hanru and Hans Ulrich Obrist.[8] The curators took as a starting point the capitalist globalization that is furiously under way in Asian countries and produced an intelligent parody of tradition as well as its conversion into commodity. The exhibition was conceived as a configuration of volatile signs that put entire cultures on offer for display and consumption, much as the accelerated market economies of East and South-East Asia promise to sustain their populaces through unruly globalization.

The two bracketing exhibitions in the foregoing discussion, *Magiciens de la Terre* and *Cities on the Move*, are examples of how curators can devise means whereby we are asked to imbibe the art experience as a swirling sea of free-floating signifiers, of how extrapolated signs are orchestrated into spectatorial affect to make up an extravagant, somewhat delirious exhibition. Such an approach can be said to have the backing of new art history (shading into cultural studies), in which the semiotic component is brought to the fore and the method of aesthetic deconstruction takes its cue (not on the basis of high art but) from the survival tactics of popular art—a tactic involving continual hybridization. This cultural and therefore aesthetic hybridity has come to stay as one of the favored curatorial approaches to exhibition-making.

I have argued that since the 80s key drives for curatorial initiative have come from exhibitions in and of the regions constituting the third world. At these sites, a range of artworks from within a chosen region are brought face-to-face with each other in order to highlight internal difference and thus to redefine received categories of ethnography and art history, ritual and theatre, material object, and concept. With overtly national-regional frames, these events have had a responsibility to fulfill and this, I believe, helps (rather than negates) a reckoning of the aesthetic presumed in western discourse to be autonomous. The foremost example is, of course, post-Mao Chinese avant-garde art: its multiple presentations in China and abroad have made it necessary to read the avant-garde intent extrapolated in alternative artistic domains in terms of the ruptures they create on the ground, the political implication of which are available in context.

Southern Biennales: 1990s Count*up*

Extending the discussion on new forums for exhibition outside the western academy and the museum of modern art, I now refer to the exponential growth of the biennials located in the south-south circuit, since these offer quite heterodox curatorial ideas.

Following the achievement of grand status by the São Paulo Biennale (begun in the 1950s), the wager for an alternative site was placed in 1986 by La Bienal de Habana (the Havana Biennale). Dedicated to third-world art (primarily from South and Central America, Africa, and Asia), the Havana Biennale projected the promise of a radical, political art into the present. No longer secure in terms of its revolutionary optimism, systematically impoverished by U.S. sanctions, outside the citadels of academic art history, beyond the hub of the Euroamerican art market, and forced to work with the most meager resources, Havana took on a vanguard role on behalf of contemporary third-world art. All the southern biennials, though each has a different agenda, owe a debt to Havana for demonstrating the potential of a decentralized art world, with alternative avant-gardes that do not need to affix a "neo." The ideological import of such an avant-garde, placed in any case off-center in respect to western canons, is noticeably *tendentious*.

Curatorially, the configuration of artworks in the Havana Biennale (I refer to its second edition, in 1989) tended to be theatrical, given that these works often came from cultures with a magic- and ritual-dominated aesthetic. But the material reality of the works' production was annotated by the simultaneous inclusion of works addressing actual politics, at least in the complex terrain of South American societies—works pointedly referring to national dictatorships and radical, subaltern movements of dissent and insurgency. These annotations were visual and textual, internal and external to the exhibition; they could also be assumed to radiate from the acute prism of the Cuban crisis and refract the terms of the global dialogue on art. Cuba is a country under siege, and its stake in cultural manifestations can be nothing less than contestatory.

Across the globe to Australia: when the Asia-Pacific Triennial was inaugurated in 1993 by the Queensland Art Gallery in Brisbane, the exhibition followed a principle already in place with Australian museums and institutional and independent curators, who consider it mandatory to put a gloss on the objects of a mixed white and aboriginal society. Consequently, in the intellectual and curatorial exercise of the Triennial, categories of the secular and the sacred had to be rethought—not with the André Malraux-*Magiciens* kind of assumption of aesthetic immanence, but in terms of the way the societies in question face these issues within a democratically organized polity. Indeed, the task was to see the way this secularization of tradition impinges on the question of citizenship in the politics of a nation. In terms of the exhibition, the secular hybrid, addressing the particular politics of a named nation, requires curatorial strategies to enable the general public to read it not only in terms of the social problematic that underlies it, but also in coeval terms with other, more familiar international art forms in the contemporary.

The point I make is this: while these multiplying biennials sometimes seem like reckless initiatives, they should be seriously scrutinized for their ironies, their follies *and* their worth.[9] Southern biennials meet with a high-handed critique—institutional fastidiousness, quality control, cultural snobbery, even open mockery—from western curators who nevertheless conduct curatorial activities at these new sites, claiming with hegemonic impunity that an international high-profile—read western—curator is essential to put the city and region in the fray on the international art map. Such biennials have sometimes been called the poor man's museum (so is the Venice Biennale the rich man's casino?), and there is some truth here. The biennial phenomenon, never beyond serving vested interests (biennials being a mixture of state spectacle, cultural hegemony, market interests, and tourist commerce), is at the same time a means of creating, through this recurring form of institutionalization, professionally charged conduits of communication in the cities and countries where biennials occur: erecting bridges between the state and private finance, between public spaces and elite enclaves, between the artists and other practitioners, including dedicated young cadres in the cultural community. The biennial can be an occasion to engage in a cognitive mapping of the culture of a region, a country, a city; at the same time, it can develop a focus on international art on home ground, the pedagogic effects of which process are enormous. This is of course especially true in countries that have no museum practice worth the name when it comes to modern and contemporary art, where the opportunities to engage with international art are scarce, and where the only "institutions" developing at breakneck pace are the art market and the auction house.[10]

The point for the new biennials is to radicalize the discourse on contemporary art toward a more contestatory position by constantly revising our understanding of the very "institution of art." Glossing the more facile skepticism that the new biennials invoke, I would like to insert the problematic into a larger polemical field, asking that we examine not just this or that biennial for its immediate certificate of excellence, but the entire relay of *site, production and discourse* in contemporary art from various vantage points on the globe.

Transnational Public Spheres

The first, second, and third worlds that defined the historical battles of the 20th century are now condensed on the principle of the new Empire that has been fully triumphant since 1989. The total interdependency among regions and nations in the economic and political spheres of global capitalism, and the heterogeneity introduced by the exchange created from the compulsions of mass migration and the consequent deterritorialization of peoples and cultures, are contrasted with the collusion of codes through the ubiquity of electronic-digital communication. A corresponding, transcultural aesthetic is not easily tracked and should be seen to be liminal, perhaps: liminal in the sense of exile, a condition in which large bodies of world citizens now subsist within and outside their communities and nations.

How is this liminality positioned in exhibition practices? At the simplest level, the inclusion of third-world (and now also second/socialist-world) artists in international exhibitions poses the diasporic in a mediatory role. Appointing *translation* as a key term, the transcultural aesthetic is supposed to stand in for the process of negotiation/confrontation between peoples. Transculturalism is not, however, a matter of free choice; it is a condition of global exchange: materially and politically coercive, if also potentially liberatory. The aesthetic that ensues requires us to come to terms with the ethical issues of violence, power, governance and citizenship implied in the new situation. It is necessary, therefore, to embed the debate in what political theorists call *transnational public spheres*—the product of contrary developments such as the emergence of post-colonial civil societies on the one hand, and of capitalist globalization on the other.

A select number of international critic-curators now write the practice of curating into discourse on the public sphere. I take one example to make my point: the 2002 *Documenta 11*, curated by Okwui Enwezor, demonstrated a new pedagogy for mapping the post-colonial global.[11] He built upon a premise he had already established in his previous exhibitions, such as the 2nd Johannesburg Biennale (1997), titled *Trade Routes: History and Geography*; and a widely toured exhibition in 2001-02 titled *The Short Century: Independence and Liberation Movements in Africa, 1945-1994*. This premise states that no discussion of critical/radical art can take place without reference to the political parameters of antagonism and redemption that come out of the decolonization process. Thus Enwezor draws on post-colonial cultural theory (in turn drawing on elements from anthropology, psychoanalysis, and a transformed Marxism) to set up new paradigms for examining representational ethics in the sphere of the symbolic—in particular, its documentary component. It also, at the same time, opens up the imaginary, thus recouping new subjectivities that claim "sovereignty" from a post-colonial status. It is Enwezor's project to determine a vantage point from which to project the subject-position of the formerly colonized, now the post-colonial citizen empowered through struggle. It is also his wager that the discourse now exists outside the national—the "original" ground where the struggle is in actual fact waged. Indeed, his faith in further transformation rests on the formation of a global citizenry with a voice in the matter of governance precisely through transnational public spheres that nurture a human and civil-rights discourse against state power. This, in Enwezor's belief, forms the utopian potential that emerges from and confronts the new Empire. Thus, with *Documenta 11* he set up a new curatorial proposition: a worldwide itinerary and a cross-disciplinary argument through a series of four discursive "platforms" that were translocated to the fifth platform, the exhibition at Kassel, where widely varying worldviews were visually sequenced into a narrative that spelled political change.

The National (as Interregnum)

My inclination is to deflect this argument[12] back to the region-nation. The site of production and exhibition is related to the form of address, and while diasporic dilemmas in the transnational arena widen the political base of the global issues tackled by art, they create another convergence. These issues are addressed to the first world—often enough in a confrontational mode—with the region and nation serving as geopolitical context. My take on these deliberately posed imponderables of identity and address is that one should move back and forth between a speculative transculturalism and a declared *partisanship* that asks how art situates itself in the still highly differentiated national economies/political societies that bear the name of countries; and how, from those sites, it reckons with divergent forces at work within globalization. More pointedly, what are the countercultural tendencies generated in the contested and contesting sites of the nations where recognizable protagonists, with well-entrenched political positions, attempt to build democratic structures of governance, institutions for a functioning civil society, and a public sphere—in opposition to, say, a neo-liberal (anti-poor) economy and/or a (covertly) authoritarian state? How do these societies organize themselves in opposition to the treacherous rule of capital and its U.S.-driven agenda, executed through monstrous wars and consumerist dystopias?

Billed under a country banner, the aura of national affiliation still works.[13] But my own experience as a critic-curator from India leads me to go beyond the sentiment, to claim that a selection of artists from a particular country/context, properly conceptualized under a theme and a problematic, can in the consequent exposition address "universal" issues of global contemporaneity (which has always been assumed to have been the case with selections of Euroamerican artists). This substantial partisanship, which goes beyond a counterbalancing polemic, should add both to art-historical knowledge and to political agendas within the discursive extension of international art.[14] Thus, for example, I want to be able to work my way through the historical trajectory and political aspiration reflected in the public sphere in India; to see how it reflects a vision (flawed, or even failed, as it might be) for a civil, democratic society, and indeed how it plays a part in determining the way the larger post-colonial, transnational public spheres are structured.

I do not want to isolate and valorize location within what is an irreversibly globalized world, but I do suggest that if contemporaneity is continually co-produced across cultures; if place, region, nation, state, and the politics of all these contextualizing categories of history (proper) are in a condition of flux everywhere in the world, we can presume past universals—regarding culture, for instance—to have been superseded, exposing the major, often lethal, tensions between peoples and regions. It is the task of specific art loci in southern countries to focus on their peculiar forms of political society that are especially volatile, and that mark a set of cultural conjunctures conducive to another kind of meaning production—in art and in history, separately and alike.

In Conclusion

It used to be said that knowledge is produced in the west, and that cultural artifacts abound in the non-west. I am inclined to invert this with a degree of caprice necessary for bold prognostications: The site for fresh discourse on the problematic of contemporaneity may be elsewhere/now here; excellence in practice is probably still a prerogative of western artists, in that the resource and knowledge of the modern tradition is theirs on command. But before this starts to sound like a familiar polemic of "us and them," I want to restore the picture of art's sovereignty within and without the institution of art, and thereby also the degree of entropy that makes the creative process and the sites of its occurrence unpredictable. The question, then, is how critic-curators can present contemporary art so as to redeem the hidden, the contextual, and also the reflexively extrapolated meanings on behalf of the artwork that is always *situated*, but also always *liminal* to the established order of things—both at once—and thus peculiarly placed to question, to be made to question via specially designed expository practices, the hegemonic tendencies of national and global, ethnic and imperialist ideologies.

My argument weaves through a series of instances to suggest how the contemporary curator's approach varies from being a collaborator, co-producing the artwork via the medium of the exhibition, to being a cultural critic, contextualizing the work through textual/visual annotation. I suggest further that these alternatives can develop more agonistic sets of relationships, where the curator stages the contradictions of the global contemporary and, acting in the manner of a friendly "enemy," makes the symbolic space the artworks inhabit more adversarial.

1. See Teresa Gleadowe, "Artist and Curator: Some Questions About Contemporary Curatorial Practice," *Visual Arts and Culture*, Volume 2, Part 1, 2000.
2. *When Attitudes Become Form* showed the work of sixty-nine artists belonging to diverse tendencies, including Conceptualism, Arte Povera, Land Art, Anti-Form, etc.: tendencies that had an avant-garde status at the time. It opened in the Bern Kunsthalle in 1969 and was later shown at the Institute of Contemporary Art in London. For Szeemann's introduction, see exhibition catalog *When Attitudes Become Form* (London: ICA, 1969).
3. In 1986, Jan Hoet curated a landmark exhibition (under the auspices of the Ghent Museum van Hedendaagse) called *Chambres d'Amis*; it spread across fifty private homes made available by the citizens to artists and visitors in what becomes a transformative act for both the production and the reception of art.
4. Seth Siegelaub, a New York gallery owner and "exhibition organizer," took the lead from the mid-1960s until 1971 with a series of exhibitions, like *The January Show* (1969). His publications-exhibitions presented Conceptual art in ways that actively supported the dematerialization of the art object and privileged the free exchange of information.
5. See *Poetics-Politics: documenta X - the book* (Ostfildern-Ruit: Cantz Verlag, 1997) for a multi-author textual compilation that complements and vastly elaborates on the premise of the curator, Catherine David.
6. The exhibition *Magiciens de la Terre* was curated by Jean-Hubert Martin for the Centre Georges Pompidou and the Musee national d'art moderne, Paris, in 1989. See exhibition catalog *Magiciens de la Terre* (Paris: Editions du Centre Pompidou, 1989).
7. The exhibition was curated by Apinan Poshyananda for the Asia Society in New York and shown in several cities. See exhibition catalog *Contemporary Art of Asia: Tradition/Tensions* (New York: Asia Society Galleries, 1996).
8. The exhibition traveled extensively through the world. See exhibition catalog *Cities on the Move* (Ostfildern-Ruit: Verlag Gerd Hatje, 1997).
9. To name some more biennials (and triennials) that began in the 1990s in the broad region of the south: the Johannesburg Biennale (started 1995, discontinued after 1997); the Kwangju Biennale (started 1995);

Dak'Art Biennial of Contemporary African Art, in Dakar (started 1996); the Shanghai Biennale (started 1996); the Taipei Biennial (started 1998). And so on. Twenty years down the line we had, in the year 2005, for instance: the 1st Moscow Biennale; the 1st Luanda Biennale, in Angola; the 2nd Yokohama International Triennale of Contemporary Art; the 2nd Beijing International Art Biennale; the 3rd Fukuoka Asian Art Triennale; the 7th Sharjah Biennale; the 8th Yogyakarta Biennale; the 9th International Istanbul Biennale; the 10th Cairo International Biennale. Among new initiatives, the Singapore Biennale follows in 2006, and there are more southern biennials in the making: for example, a group of independent critics, curators, and artists set up a platform in January 2005 to launch the project for a Delhi Biennale that can supersede the now moribund Delhi Triennale started in 1968.

10. Charles Merewether, art historian, curator, and artistic director of the 2006 Biennale of Sydney (*Zones of Contact*), spoke in January 2005 at a New Delhi conference (titled "The Making of International Exhibitions: Siting Biennales") about biennials as sites where experiments with unlikely simultaneities in crosscultural artworks are presented, and also where an interrogation of contemporaneity, as such, is conducted using a methodology drawn from advanced cultural theory in tune with the rapidly changing political contexts around the globe. Museums of modern and contemporary art, on the other hand, are bound by institutional, still conservative frames of western art history and belong within what Charles Esche, co-curator of the 9th International Istanbul Biennale (2005), speaking at a conference (titled "Biennalicity") at the time of the 7th Sharjah Biennale (2005), designated as the bourgeois public sphere. Quoting Chantal Mouffe (*The Democratic Paradox*), Esche spoke about the *spirit of agonism*—a relation between adversaries, friendly enemies, who share a common symbolic space and contest different forms of its organization. He suggested that the emerging series of "planetary" biennials can contribute to a reciprocal critique of the two institutions—the museum framed by the (western) bourgeois public sphere, and the biennial, a spectacular eventlike manifestation within transcultural exchange, or what other curators, like Okwui Enwezor, consider to be the *post-colonial* transnational public sphere. (Proceedings of both conferences remain unpublished.)

11. See introduction by Enwezor and texts by the Documenta team and other authors, in *Documenta 11_Platform 5: Exhibition Catalogue* (Ostfildern-Ruit: Hatje Cantz Publishers, 2002). Preceding the exhibition, the *Documenta 11* team conducted a set of symposia (Platforms 1-4) in Vienna, New Delhi, St. Lucia/Carribean, and Lagos, each published as a book (Ostfildern-Ruit: Hatje Cantz Publishers, 2002): *Democracy Unrealized*; *Experiments with Truth: Transitional Justice and the Processes of Truth and Reconciliation*; *Creolité and Creolization*; and *Under Siege: Four African Cities, Freetown, Johannesburg, Kinshasa, and Lagos*.

12. See Geeta Kapur, *When Was Modernism: Essays on Contemporary Cultural Practice in India* (New Delhi: Tulika Books, 2000), in which I deal with the uneven/anomalous nature of third-world modernisms, and how this leads on to differently periodized, differently theorized, variously located avant-garde moments, and thence to styles and strategies of expository presentation.

13. Incidentally, Szeemann was led to say about national pavilions, in an interview with Jan Winkelmann titled "Failure as a Poetic Dimension. A Conversation with Harald Szeemann" (published in *Metropolis M. Tijdschrift over hedendaagse kunst*, No. 3, June 2001): "And of course you had the eternal discussion again about whether to abolish the national pavilions or not. I find these national presentations of utmost importance. The outstanding chance for Biennales like those of Venice and São Paulo is that they have these two foundations, the national and the international. Precisely through this combination you can then build bridges, and that's where the challenge of the Biennale model lies." As it happens, the national sections have been abolished in the São Paulo Biennale of 2006.

14. I was asked by the Tate Modern in London to conceptualize and curate an exposition referring to the visual culture of an Indian city for what was to become its inaugural, multipart exhibition, *Century City: Art and Culture in Modern Metropolis* (2001). The dynamic of art and visual culture at specific points in the 20th century was sought to be brought into focus by nine city-sections—Paris, Vienna, Moscow, Rio de Janeiro, Lagos, Tokyo, New York, Bombay and London. This involved not simply a choice of a decade or of a political moment, but of a historical conjuncture in the 20th century. Working with the film theorist Ashish Rajadhyaksha as co-curator, I selected Bombay in the 1990s as a signature 20th century metropolis. (See Geeta Kapur and Ashish Rajadhyaksha, "Bombay/Mumbai: 1992-2001," *Century City: Art and Culture in the Modern Metropolis*, exhibition catalog, edited by Iwona Blazwick (London: Tate Publishing, 2001)). We focused on its peculiar dynamic, pitching it not simply as a local cultural variation on the theme of the modern, but a demonstration of the co-production of modernities at different sites, national and metropolitan. We looked for the consequences of these processes as they force their way into contemporary history: from policy-driven economic choices to forms (and distortions) in the democratic functioning of urban space, to the peculiar characteristics of its citizenry and the public sphere it supports. Indeed, far from being merely a case study of *difference*, historicization of this kind constitutes the very definition of the 20th century from

which neither the cultural nor the political imaginary of the white-western, first-world citizen can escape. While some of the work was specially produced for the exhibition, the contextualizing gained by working at the exhibition's spatial design and, more important, the discursive extrapolation on the peculiar form of the Indian metropolis, guided the curatorial approach.

Geeta Kapur is an independent art critic and curator living in Delhi. Her writings on art and cultural theory are widely anthologized; her books include *Contemporary Indian Artists* (New Delhi, 1978) and *When was Modernism: Essays on Contemporary Cultural Practice in India* (New Delhi, 2000). Her more recent curatorial work includes a co-curated show, *Bombay/Mumbai 1992-2001*, in the multi-part exhibition, *Century City: Art and Culture in the Modern Metropolis* (Tate Modern, London, 2001); and *subTerrain* (House of World Cultures, Berlin, 2003). She served on the International Jury of the 51st Venice Biennale, 2005. One of the founder-editors of *Journal of Arts & Ideas*, she is advisory editor to *Third Text* and *Marg*. She has lectured world-wide and held Fellowships at the Indian Institute of Advanced Study, Shimla; Clare Hall, University of Cambridge; Nehru Memorial Museum and Library, Delhi; the University of Delhi, and the Jawaharlal Nehru University, Delhi.

András Szántó

Editing as Metaphor

On November 9, 1895, the British humor magazine *Punch* published a cartoon by George du Maurier of a curate breakfasting in the company of his bishop. In the Anglican Church, a "curate" was a holder of a junior ecclesiastical rank, such as an assistant to a rector or a vicar. In the cartoon, the bishop declares, "I'm afraid you've got a bad egg, Mr. Jones." The curate's exquisitely hedged answer: "Oh, no, my Lord, I assure you that parts of it are excellent."

The cartoon was popular among readers, and the phrase "parts of it are excellent" caught on. It gave rise to a new expression in the English language of a "curate's egg," which was taken to mean something that is partly good and partly bad, and therefore not altogether satisfactory. "This book is a bit of a curate's egg" is a kind of line you might hear on *Masterpiece Theatre*. Today, in the art world, the task of choosing between the parts that are bad and the parts that are excellent falls to a profession whose members are distantly related to the equivocating cleric in the cartoon. This profession has sometimes been likened to priesthood. And it, too, has a complicated relationship with authority.

The word "curator" has been around for more than 600 years. At first, it referred to an "overseer" or a "guardian," notably of minors and lunatics. Its root stems from the Latin "curare," which means to take care of something. Dictionaries since the mid-17th century have defined "curator" as an "officer in charge of a museum, library, etc." Most of the etymological connotations of the word apply to curators working today. To curate, above all, is to be curious ("curiositas" is "inquisitiveness"). To curate is to nurture and to protect ("curatorio" means "attention" and "healing"). And to curate is to be well organized ("curo" means "to manage, administer"). These qualities have enabled curators of private and, later, public collections to preserve the beautiful and "curious" objects in their keep and arrange them into configurations that achieve a desired visual or educational effect.

Today, it's no exaggeration to say that we're living in a golden age of the curator. Never have curators been so profuse in number or so necessary to bringing order into the affairs of art. When it comes to contemporary art, this job of sense-making belongs more and more to the so-called "independent curator," a recent arrival on the art-world stage whose duties and qualifications are still being clarified. For independent curators especially, thorny questions follow from the definitions above: Overseer or guardian of what? Curious in which direction? Protector in whose name? Organizer in keeping with what sorts of principles? As the art world grows, and curators accumulate power and visibility, the answers turn fuzzier.

In fact, the term "curator" lumps together various activities and priorities that can seem quite incompatible. It is probably no less misleading to call anyone who organizes exhibitions a curator than to call anyone who sells art a dealer. The museum curator works on the staff of a single institution and is charged with studying, building, displaying, and caring for its collection. The just mentioned independent curator organizes temporary exhibitions in museums, galleries, and other venues on a free-lance basis. A third type is a dealer, who puts together shows with the ultimate purpose of selling works and realizing a profit. A fourth is a critic, who broadens the purview of art writing through conceptualizing and facilitating exhibitions. Several of these roles can blend together in the career path of a single individual. And to them we may add another figure that has gained notoriety of late: the collector-curator, who executes a sort of curatorial strategy through his pattern of acquisitions, and may display his collection in his own exhibition venue. Some might find certain of these variations on the role of the curator less agreeable than others. But in the vast, commercialized and professionalized art world of our day, all sorts of explainers and intermediaries are being inserted between the makers and "consumers" of art.

For anyone hoping to make a life out of organizing exhibitions, it is worth reflecting on a few dilemmas associated with certain aspects of curating. A persistent challenge for museum curators is maintaining their sense of balance and integrity in the face of organizational and logistical impediments that can derail even the best-laid plans for building a collection or an exhibition. Museums, like all large institutions, gravitate toward a state of bureaucratic insularity. Life inside the bubble is subject to incessant trade-offs and compromises, from the whims of capricious directors to the poker games being played with collectors to secure loans and bequests.

Successful curators are virtuosos of the art of institutional politics. The first mistake an aspiring curator could make, inside or outside a museum, is to expect a life in an ivory tower, in lofty pursuit of pure aesthetics. Good exhibitions come together through deft negotiation of artistic priorities and institutional realities.

The connection of dealing and curating raises questions about art and commerce, words that always imply a tension when placed side by side. Some large galleries are, for the casual visitor, virtually indistinguishable from museums. They provide a kind of public service by mounting ambitious, well-documented shows, sometimes with the help of invited curators. But the blurring of boundaries between curating and art dealing carries risks. Art dealers are in business to sell art. No matter how "academic" a gallery's front room may be, its function is to support sales—and there is nothing wrong with that. Galleries should be applauded for funding curatorial projects. The problems happen when the line between the artistic and the commercial aspects of the enterprise begins to fade. It becomes hard to tell where the educational effort ends and where the selling begins. Curators who take on assignments in galleries must be mindful of their autonomy. They need to be honest with themselves about their role in the art market. The real issue is not engagement with commerce—all but inevitable in today's art world—but the market's uncanny ability to sway judgment. It's hard not to be influenced by the market's choices about which art is bad and which is excellent. Those rankings, expressed in the blunt clarity of prices, are most seductive, and usually misleading. Rubber-stamping the fashionable consensus is a trap curators must assiduously avoid.

It is fair to say, paraphrasing Carl von Clausewitz, that a curator's work is an extension of criticism by other means. Some of our most influential curators are also critics. The question is whether criticism and what is loosely called "theory" can still provide a sturdy foundation for curatorial practices. Unfortunately, for a number of reasons, curating has lost some of the energy and inspiration it once received from this important source. In a perfect world, criticism and curating would function in unison, as two sides of a coin. But criticism is nowadays hobbled by a lack of intellectual direction, not to mention a stultifying obscurantism. The waning of the major 20th century philosophical paradigms has left behind a void. No new big and widely assimilated ideas have emerged to serve as a compass for the art world. The resulting pluralism of today's art is undeniably liberating, but also confusing: If anything goes, what should be the role of the critic or the curator as an arbiter of values? And if there are no widely accepted benchmarks of merit, how should anyone tell the bad art from the excellent?

Contemporary art exhibitions all too often manifest this malaise. As I'll elaborate later, they are prone to jargon, bloat, and hair-splitting—escape hatches that help critics avoid normative statements of merit and direction. Today's "aesthetics of uncertainty," to borrow Janet Wolff's precisely evocative phrase, have introduced a degree of uncertainty and wishy-washiness into curatorial efforts as well.

What we are beginning to see, in fact, is a 21st century reappraisal of critical judgment. It's a shift in attitude that has serious implications for curators. A few years ago, a group of critics was asked in a survey about which aspects of reviewing they emphasized in their work. The options included writing well, theorizing, rendering a personal opinion, contextualizing, and describing the exhibited objects at hand. It turns out that the dimension of reviewing that critics emphasize the *least* is "rendering a personal judgment or opinion." In other words, the act of judging has become problematic in a world in which dominant paradigms and more or less universally held ideas have gone out of fashion. "The days of the chest-thumping oracle critic are over," one of the surveyed critics observed.

But if no clear reasons are available to justify distinctions between the bad art and the excellent, from where should a curator's choices derive? This is a worrisome dilemma. One would certainly hope that curatorial discernment rests on sturdier foundations than fashion, whimsy, personal infatuations, and vendettas, or a vague sense of what connects to what. Art can come from the gut, but a curator's work should begin, at least in part, in the head. It seems to me that along with the pluralism of today's art must come a less heavy-handed approach to thinking about art and, correspondingly, a more nuanced outlook on curating. But this cannot mean that we abandon the notion that some artworks or artists are better than others. The point is that curators today have a responsibility to find new, more legitimate ways of negotiating some kind of consensus about art. It's okay to say that values are provisional, but you still need a method for figuring out what really matters. Such agreement ought to be based not on imposed and exclusive ideas about merit, but on some kind of process that absorbs a wider array of influences and viewpoints. This is a tall order. On the one hand, you're supposed to broaden the acceptable range of perspectives and expressions. On the other hand, you're supposed to make justifiable choices. Nobody said this was going to be easy.

Intelligent curators will always be mindful of the treacherous institutional landscape in which they work, the awkward and sometimes corrupting tensions between art and commerce that can undermine their best efforts, and the shifting critical ground on which their enterprise rests. But the purpose of this essay is to offer practical advice. Not being a curator, I'll leave guidance about the technical parts of the job to others. From here forward, I will focus on the parts of the curator's enterprise that bring order and meaning into the affairs of art. I will illustrate the challenges through a field whose customs I know reasonably well, and whose dilemmas turn out to have much in common with curating. I'm talking about editors.

The rules of editing are relevant for two reasons. First, because most curators write—and judging by what they usually write, a refresher about some principles of editing might be useful. More important, editors are, in a very real sense, curators—curators of texts and writers—and it stands to reason that insights from one field would apply in the other. So what can curators learn from editors?

Know a good story: The hallmark of a good editor is the ability to spot a story. No amount of linguistic virtuosity or editorial zeal can substitute for a plot. Part of knowing a story is recognizing the form it should take. Some stories want to be long; others need to stay short. Some demand an air of detachment; others profit from a personal point of view. There are stories so overloaded with detail that they risk collapsing under their own weight; these need to be unpacked. Others are so splintered and granular that it is impossible to see the point; these must be tightened. It is easy to see how these editorial objectives translate into the design of exhibitions. We have all visited shows that are too detailed or too short, too opinionated or too dry. A good curator, like a good editor, knows that such problems are due in part to how the material is presented to the audience. Storytelling is the shared art of the curator and the editor. Good storytelling can correct situations when a story has too many characters or too few. It calls for a sense of rhythm, pacing, and the courage to send stuff to the cutting-room floor. A good storyteller is, above all, a master of exposition. She can massage a text until it flows, revealing the plot bit by bit, keeping the audience hungry, knowing when to add pauses, humor, or surprise, and saving some of the best for last. Too many exhibitions tell stories that should never be told, are told too early or too late, or simply are told badly, rambling aimlessly in search of a plot. My favorite shows are those with a clear narrative structure. Dynamic plotlines are readily available: documentations of artistic collaboration or competition, narratives of individual growth or decline, evolutionary chronicles that lead from obscurity to cultural triumph, closely observed accounts of the emergence of a particular artistic group, and so on. If a curator has a grip on the story, the battle is half won.

Aim for concision: "Less is more" is the credo of a good editor. This is rarely heeded by curators (or writers, for that matter).

Eliminate bloat: As every editor knows, too much text can smother the message of the author (who is usually his own worst enemy in this respect). Curators often lavish repetitive or extraneous material on exhibitions. They cram in too much, I suspect, because they only have one shot at telling the story; opportunities to assemble a group of artists or a particular group of works don't come around often. Some exhibitions, decades in the making, are career-capping feats of research and organizational virtuosity. It's understandable when a curator, like a zealous recruit at a job interview, gets carried away and ends up saying too much. (Think of those ponderous retrospectives that begin with tentative drawings from the artist's youth, linger at length on every stage of his life's journey, and reverently display unfinished, sometimes embarrassing pictures from his twilight years.) Bloat can stem from the well-meaning impulse to be comprehensive, to acknowledge minor players in larger stories, or to pay respect to diversity. There is always a seemingly valid reason. Restraint, under these circumstances, is a paramount virtue. Exhibit A, when it comes to curatorial bloat—and an ironic one, in this age of information overload—is the mega-blockbuster, with its cinderblock-size catalog. Monuments to megalomania, these elephantine productions are not so much exhaustive as exhausting. The bottom line: one lesson editors can teach curators is how to say no.

Avoid hair-splitting: Every writer has come across that most annoying editor: the kind who asks too many questions, inserts too many commas, queries too many facts, and frets constantly about "what we're saying." The hair-splitter cannot accept a story simply for what it is. For the hair-splitter, an otherwise fine idea may seem too general or too narrow, too trendy or not trendy enough, too plainspoken or lacking a strong voice. Such nitpicking undermines the message without helping the story. Hair-splitters are obsessed with technique, presentation, and style. Their labors amount to death by a thousand niggling details. In journalism, their motto is "Why should the reader care?" Wet blankets in the art world ask, "Is this our kind of show?" "Does the audience want to see this?" "Why does this belong in a museum?" "Didn't another gallery do this five years ago?" Pedantic curators operate more by fear than instinct. Their caution leads them to conceive exhibitions too rarified to be of interest to a wide audience. The best editors and curators rise above details and make big bets. Hair-splitters freak out when objects deemed unworthy of serious attention (such as motorcycles) appear in a museum or art gallery. Their aversion to stretching boundaries can lead to missed opportunities.

Resist forced ideas: There is a rule of thumb in journalism that is encapsulated in the phrase "three makes a trend." In other words, if a reporter can find three examples of a phenomenon, it can be written about as a trend. The rule has some merit. If a writer on deadline can find three examples of anything, there is probably something going on out there. But sometimes three doesn't make a trend—not even close. A good editor has an eye for spotting genuinely relevant developments, and so it goes for curators. Many alleged art trends are intellectual fabrications foisted upon art by critics and historians. Others are marketing gimmicks invented by dealers and collectors (these often come with groovy titles to suggest something even grander than a trend—a movement). Certain trend-like phenomena, while strictly speaking real, are too obvious or vacuous to deserve serious consideration. Recent years, for example, have seen a vogue for large photography, but an exhibition solely devoted to large photographs would be asinine. Looking back at the 1980s, we see a graveyard of artistic fads and fashions that came and went in a flash and are hardly remembered today.

Forced ideas happen in curating when some kind of rationale has to be invented for putting together a group of artists or objects. The seemingly unavoidable pressure to dish up extravaganzas devoted to Impressionists has, for example, given rise to countless museum exhibitions expounding on transparently forced themes. The thing to remember is that forced ideas, bloat, and the absence of a plot form a sort of trinity—one compels the other. Curators, much like writers and editors, paper over the absence of a storyline by heaping more and more stuff into the picture. Bloat thus aims to obscure the weakness of the trend proposition. How to spot an empty trend? By an indecipherable title. Provocatively titled group shows tempt you with a frisson of trend-spotting, but on close inspection, they invariably lack a unifying theme.

Stamp out jargon: Jargon is like a pox on good writing. It deposits scar tissue all over the story and leaves permanent damage. It must be eradicated at all costs. Jargon-besotted writing is indelibly linked to fuzzy curating, and both seem to resist all attempts to find a cure. The culprits are well known. First came academic credentializing of writers and artists. Then Modernism imploded, leaving a residue of uncertainty about art's purpose and direction. Last but not least, most art writing is commissioned directly from writers and rarely put to the test of a popular readership. Art, to be sure, deserves the support of complex ideas. But the tolerance for gobbledygook in today's art world is stultifying. Intellectual intimidation has something to do with it, but this epidemic of incomprehensibility is also linked, oddly enough, to the commercialization of art. Astronomical prices demand a smokescreen of "theory" around objects whose monetary value has no material basis in objective reality.

My point is not just that curators should avoid writing or commissioning bewilderingly complicated texts, but that they need to be careful about putting on exhibitions that are physical embodiments of abstruse theories. Just sanitizing wall texts, that most basic form of communication with the audience, would be a major achievement. Jargon, it is worth noting, is closely related in its pretentiousness and disorienting effect to colloquialism. (Preoccupation with youth culture is widespread everywhere in society, and nowhere more so than in contemporary art.) But while jargon and colloquialism are kissing cousins, they stem from different roots. Colloquialism is a relatively minor nuisance that feeds on a juvenile urge to be trendy and cool. Jargon, by contrast, is rooted in fear—the fear of having nothing to say. Curators have a special responsibility in the struggle against jargon. They are the first responders. But some are abetting the enemy.

Other insights gleaned from the world of editing, such as "know your grammar" and "understand that group editing leads to disaster," have recognizable analogies in a curator's life. A basic knowledge of history and the methods of art making is indispensable, and "groupthink"—especially when marketers and fundraisers are involved—is directly responsible for some of the symptoms of bad curating outlined above. However, there is an area where the crossover between editing and curating is less obvious. Editors have clearer principles to fall back on when it comes to maintaining the integrity of the creative process against institutional and commercial encroachments.

In the American newsroom, this is called the "church and state" problem, and it is a matter of contention and constant negotiation. And that is a very healthy thing. Journalism, especially daily journalism, is miles ahead of the art world in maintaining barriers between the content side and the business side of the enterprise. Procedures are in place governing everything from accepting gifts to maintaining a firewall between advertisers and writers (some papers have ombudsmen to enforce such rules). To be sure, the barriers between content and business are tumbling in many precincts of journalism, but the basic rules of conduct are much clearer for everyone involved. Curators and the institutions that employ them still have a lot of fuzzy areas to sort out in the realm of professional ethics.

The ethical norms governing the art world have, by and large, resisted codification. They are recognized and imposed mainly through a process of trial and error. On the whole, curators are left to their own devices when it comes to making arrangements with donors, collectors, other museums, and commercial entities. Meltdowns like the "Sensation" controversy at the Brooklyn Museum of Art or the recent dustup at the Getty Museum are the inevitable result of this lack of clarity. These crises inflict a great deal of damage, sometimes even paralysis, especially when pumped up by a scandal-hungry press. And when they do happen, they can no longer be dealt with quietly, behind the scenes. Transparency is now the rule even for society's most sacrosanct institutions. The last piece of advice I would offer, therefore, to curators embarking on their careers is to make it their priority to develop clear and consistent operating guidelines for themselves and their profession. They will help you when the going gets tough.

It is unlikely that these principles would fit into a slim rulebook, suitable for carrying around in a purse or vest pocket. As in all matters ethical, much will depend on a curator's own judgment and common sense. The essence of professionalism is a constant negotiation of what is or is not acceptable for a project, an institution, or an expert field. Gray areas will always remain. It is important to remember that the art world is not a holy sanctuary that floats above everyday reality, exempt from its rules; nor is it a corrupt and cynical sham that rewards only those with sharp elbows and winning looks. In the end, here as elsewhere, those who do well are the ones who stay honest, do their homework, remember their friends, and keep their feet on the ground.

So what should young curators expect of their profession? Well, I guess you could say it is a bit of a curate's egg. Parts of a curator's life will always be good, but it will never be altogether satisfactory. Other jobs reward the same skill and preparation with more prestige or money. Dealing with artists, collectors, museums, and the myriad details of mounting exhibitions will lead to headaches. Even so, within the art world, things are looking up. In a time when artists are producing new work in unprecedented numbers, launching a myriad museum and gallery shows and a rash of annuals, biennials, and arts fairs; and when criticism no longer provides a proper road map for navigating this jungle of amplified activity, curators—especially the independent, unaffiliated, globetrotting kind—stand to achieve greater prominence.

We may be at a turning point. The century-long reign of the gallery-critic system appears to be drawing to a close. The first versions of art history are no longer being written exclusively through gallery shows and reviews. In the pluralized, globalized, de-centered art world of our moment, the crucial dynamics are being determined by aggregators—auctions, art fairs, and biennials. The reason is simple: the art world and art market have become so huge, stretching across so many disciplines, cities, and continents, that taking it all in morsel by morsel, gallery show by gallery show, critical review by critical review, no longer makes sense. Wider and deeper webs of connections have to be proposed for this vastness to cohere into a manageable, fathomable whole. Money, the universal equalizer, will continue to claim the spotlight. But when it comes to substance—to helping us comprehend it all—curators will discover a new mandate to shape the story of art.

The author wishes to express his gratitude to the American Academy in Rome, where sections of this essay were written.

András Szántó writes frequently on the worlds of art, media, and cultural affairs. He is a member of the senior faculty of the Sotheby's Institute of Art in New York. He is a Senior Advisor to the Wealth & Giving Forum, Director of the NEA Arts Journalism Institute at Columbia University, and a Visiting Scholar at New York University. Among his previous appointments, he was a Marian and Andrew Heiskell Visiting Critic at the American Academy in Rome and Director of the National Arts Journalism Program at Columbia, where he oversaw numerous studies on arts and media, including *The Visual Art Critic: A Survey of Art Critics at General-Interest News Publications in America*. His reporting and commentary have appeared in *The New York Times, The Boston Globe, Los Angeles Times, The American Prospect, Newsday, Interiors, Architecture, Print, I.D., The Art Newspaper, International Herald Tribune, Variety*, and other newspapers and periodicals.

David Carrier

Why Curators Matter

> Perspectivism does not result in the relativism that holds that any view is as good as any other; it...generates the expectation that new views and values are bound to become necessary as it produces the willingness to develop and to accept such new schemes...
>
> Alexander Nehamas[1]

In Giorgio Vasari's Florence, Nicolas Poussin's Rome, and Denis Diderot's and Charles Baudelaire's Paris, there were no curators. Nor were curators found in the sophisticated traditional visual cultures of China, India, or the Islamic world. But Roger Fry was a curator. He organized in London a pioneering exhibition of French Post-Impressionism. The anarchist art writer Félix Fénénon played an important role in Henri Matisse's career. Clement Greenberg worked as a curator from December 1958 until February 1960, advising French and Company about what contemporary artists to exhibit.[2] And Arthur Danto has curated several exhibitions, including a recent show responding to 9/11 at apexart. Curators are creations of, and very distinctive products of, the modern bourgeois market in art.

Once there are many exciting living artists, gifted curators are needed to locate and present them persuasively to the public. And sometimes curators support scholarship by staging exhibitions, which test important theories of contemporary art. Robert Rauschenberg's early silkscreen paintings were used by Douglas Crimp to stage an influential theory of post-Modernism. And so the 1991 exhibition at the Whitney, which demonstrated the obvious implausibility of Crimp's claims, was revelatory.[3] Curators also play an important role in defining and revising taste in older art. Thanks in part to intelligent championship by Alfred Barr and John Elderfield, Henri Matisse has a deservedly exalted position in the American art world. Roberto Longhi's famously influential exhibition in Milan, in 1951, was vital to the revival of Caravaggio's reputation. Recent feminist scholars have devoted a great deal of attention to Artemisia Gentileschi, and so the large survey at the Metropolitan in

2002, *Orazio and Artemisia Gentileschi: Father and Daughter Painters in Baroque Italy*, played an important role in introducing these scholarly concerns to the public.

In one significant way, curators can potentially have more influence than art historians. Only a minority of Americans study art history, and only a relatively small percentage of college students go beyond the introductory survey courses. But everyone who visits museums sees the curators' interpretations. And so, because art museums are extremely popular public spaces, strong exhibitions have great educational potential. Successful curators are mediators, standing between artists and their public. They have wide art world contacts, a point of view, and the skill needed to present their visual analysis in effective, crowd-pleasing exhibitions.

In citing my own reviews as evidence in this essay, I merely offer one critic's perspective. As my epigraph from Alexander Nehamas suggests, other perspectives are available. Many of my claims are highly controversial. And like every critic, I can be highly subjective. Now and then I support friends whose art is not taken seriously by the mainstream media or criticize artists almost everyone else admires. Such personal judgments can readily inspire controversy, which is, I think, a good thing. If curators do not express strong opinions, they merely tell us what we already know. Salander O'Reilly Gallery in New York City consistently presents exhibitions of modernist and contemporary art that challenge received ideas about taste. Seeing its recent displays of Graham Nickson, Paul Resika, and Stone Roberts, to mention just three of its artists who interest me, should inspire serious reflection about the usual academic narratives of modernism.[4]

When you are a young curator dealing with contemporary art, then you need to find some artist or group of artists that you care about and present them. And you should discover a style of visual thinking that you believe deserves attention. There is no need to worry about being objective, for there are many opposing critical forces at work within our Darwinian art world. If your artists are bores and your ways of thinking dull, then soon enough they will be discarded. Most often, critics and curators respond most easily to art made by near contemporaries. And so as you become middle-aged, it is important to look at younger artists, for otherwise you will never broaden your early tastes. There is something pathetic about aging commentators who fail to do that, as in the case of Harold Rosenberg, who endlessly praised Willem de Kooning—and told us that since the golden age of his youth, the art world had gone to hell. The American art world depends upon the generally shared belief that very exciting new artists will continue to emerge. Young curators need, then, to be of their time.

In our art world, where museums need large audiences to pay their bills, there is an obvious tension between satisfying the larger public and pleasing critical reviewers. The blockbuster show *Russia!* (fall 2005 at the Guggenheim in New York) attracted enormous crowds with a very problematic selection of pictures.[5] Along with some fascinating icons and a number of important Constructivist paintings, the display included a great deal of socialist-realism kitsch. To see the important paintings, you needed to walk past a great deal of dull art. Better, I think, for a curator to be admired by his or her peers than to achieve this kind of inherently problematic public success. Just as historians tend to focus attention on the most famous artists, and not their forgotten rivals, so with curators' shows one most remembers the success stories, not the failures. The very effective presentation of Robert Ryman by Robert Storr at the Museum of Modern Art in 1993 effectively consolidated Ryman's reputation.[6] A large Kunsthalle exhibit of Alex Katz in 1998 played a similar role.[7] And a show at the Metropolitan the same year devoted to Pierre-Paul Prud'hon, who until then was too little known in America, was a revelation.[8]

But many ambitious exhibitions fail, and the study of them can be extremely instructive. The large claims made for R. B. Kitaj did not survive his large museum exhibition at the Hirshhorn in 1982.[9] And a very large show of Ellsworth Kelly's paintings at the Guggenheim in 1996 demonstrated that he is a gifted but limited artist.[10] When serious claims are made for mid-career artists, museum exhibitions permit reality-testing. Cai Gou-Qiang is much admired, but his show at Mass MoCa in the fall of 2004 was a noisy disaster.[11] Jim Hodges, by contrast, was an artist whose Cleveland exhibition in 2005 revealed real strengths.[12] His art, one learned, was subtle and varied. Until you see a body of an artist's works, you cannot predict whether a large exhibition will be a success.

Survey shows linking together artists in novel ways may be suggestive, but are often problematic.[13] When, in 1981 at the Los Angeles Institute of Contemporary Art, a Los Angeles curator linked Andy Warhol with Leroy Neiman, the famous illustrator who is not taken seriously in the art world, that show did not elevate Neiman.[14] By contrast, an exhibit in 1999 at the Kimbell Museum in Fort Worth, Texas, that pitted Matisse against Picasso effectively demonstrated how the rivalry of these artists fueled their careers.[15] In the late 1980s and early 1990s many group shows were devoted to abstract painting. In 1991, for example, John Good Gallery in New York presented Demetrio Paparoni's *La metafisica della luce* and Sidney Janis Gallery, also in New York, hosted *Conceptual Abstraction*, curated by Carroll Janis.

Some of the artists in these shows went on to have important careers, but on the whole these attempts to demonstrate that contemporary abstraction was a significant movement failed completely.[16] One obvious problem was that no one had an interesting theory of this painting. Another difficulty was that such exhibitions seemed to extend Greenberg's basic way of thinking at a time when most critics felt very strongly that formalism had finally been exhausted.

Curating is an exercise in visual rhetoric. What the art writer does in texts, projecting an interpretation and so getting us to see in a new way, the curator does with the works of art themselves.[17] Just as a writer assembles a group of illustrations to display the development of art, or indicate visual affinities, a curator achieves the same effect by putting together an exhibition. And so, to pursue this parallel, just as such a writer's arguments can fail to match your visual experience, so the same may happen when a curator's claims do not inspire conviction. An enormous exhibit in 2000 at the Los Angeles Museum of Art tried, and failed, to identify an interesting shared sensibility of California artists.[18] When curators make large claims for marginal artists, critics need to be wary. Patti Smith is a wonderful rock performer but not, as her show at the Warhol Museum in Pittsburgh in 2002 demonstrated, a convincing visual artist.[19] Similarly, Jean Cocteau—whose show also was at the Warhol, in 2001—was a fascinating writer and personality, but not an artist whose drawings deserve a museum retrospective.[20]

Often there is a concern about curators' conflicts of interest. When a critic champions an artist or a group of artists, inevitably he or she promotes these figures. A show in a small gallery can help initiate an artist's career, and a large museum retrospective will surely promote sales. And so artists, who are grateful for attention, often give art to their supporters. If you are a young critic or curator, then it is natural to accept gifts or to purchase at low prices works of art you admire. Serious gifts from more senior artists are another matter. Once art has exchange value, then giving it to a curator is like handing over cash. I once watched a curator accept a painting from an artist whose show he had just presented at a great New York museum. That, I think, is bribery. Some collectors seek advice from curators in shameless ways. Because American museums depend so heavily upon private funding, there is real pressure upon curators to do favors for super-rich collectors. My hunch is that this is an especial problem in provincial cities, where a few personalities can dominate the scene. Traditionally, some very rich people have supported the arts generously. One hopes that a collector who is grateful for good advice will support the curator's museum, but that may not happen. Curators should be aware that nowadays very many collectors treat art as a form of speculative investment, and will quickly sell to make a profit.[21]

These qualifications aside, moralizing about the art world usually seems to me misplaced. Art world politics is not the same thing as real world politics, where moralizing is entirely appropriate. Like everyone except those happy few who are lucky enough to have trust funds, curators need to make a living. And in the art-world system of exchange, in which we all take up roles, curators, like critics, dealers and artists, need to support themselves.[22] You cannot really be entirely objective in this situation, for the price of admission to the community is the desire to influence commentary. And so there is no reason not to act on your taste, however subjective it may seem. After all, when you are dead, posterity will judge your claims. If you produce great shows, no one will worry about how they were financed. But if your exhibitions are forgotten, then no one will care.

If you become a curator, especially a high-profile curator, it is best that you have a thick skin. When the Carnegie Internationals or the Whitney Biennials present just fifty or eighty artists, arguing that these are the most challenging living figures, inevitably such choices provoke envy. Many tens of thousands of artists have been left out, and, naturally, they will be resentful. My experience is that these shows are very hard to review for just this reason. One is readily aware that the announced theme does not adequately describe the art on display.[23] What really is on display is the curator's taste. And when the Museum of Modern Art puts on a grand show of one senior artist, inevitably his or her peers ask why they have not been shown. Shows devoted to masterpieces by Matisse or Picasso are relatively uncontroversial, but once we get to living artists, large exhibitions inevitably will be controversial.

I am a great admirer of Sean Scully, whose central goal, extending the tradition of Abstract Expressionism, is highly controversial.[24] I know one curator who never took Scully seriously until an extremely influential patron gave a major gift to his museum. This person's newly proclaimed interest in Scully depressed me. Better, I believe, to have real opinions than to merely align yourself with what is going on. Recently Elizabeth Murray and Gerhard Richter have had major retrospectives at the Museum of Modern Art. But not everyone thinks that they are great artists. I find them interesting but not canonical figures. Many other critics would of course take violent exception to these claims. One important function of large museum exhibits is to allow us to judge for ourselves.

The critic I feel closest to is Arthur Danto. We admire some of the same artists, but also often have real disagreements about taste. Danto dislikes Poussin, whom I have written a book about, and admires passionately some living artists who bore me.[25] I love our disagreements, for how dull art-world life would be if we always agreed with our friends. One famous New York curator, who regularly engages in public confrontations with his critics, is unable to admit what ought to be obvious: that in the contemporary art world there often are serious and entirely legitimate debates about taste. Critical judgments tend to be delivered in a dogmatic way, but when we get to art after Abstract Expressionism, the canon has not been established. In their recent large survey history, Hal Foster, Rosalind Krauss, Yve-Alain Bois and Benjamin Buchloh, collectively the most influential living American critics, do not include Chuck Close, Sam Francis or Robert Mangold.[26] Their perspective has of course been immediately challenged.

Having made the best case possible for the artists he admires, the curator would do best to retire from the scene, knowing that if his claims are challenging, they will provoke controversy. Much can be learned about the role of curators as advocates by considering the career of Clement Greenberg. Often one reads complaints about his power over curators. But unlike political dictators, Greenberg was just a writer whose opinions curators could take or leave. If you did not believe that Jackson Pollock was a great artist, or that Jules Olitski was his heir, no harm came to you if you expressed that dissent. A dictator has real power, but a curator has only the power given by his or her audience. When William Rubin presented Greenberg's basic way of thinking as curator at the Museum of Modern Art, nothing prevented critics from dissenting. Indeed, that museum now has rejected Rubin's vision of art history.

A curator can offer a perspective, but only the art-world consensus can validate any one person's point of view. In the end, an artist's reputation depends upon this consensus, which is to say that no single curator or group of curators dominate our art world. Frank Stella had many powerful champions, and he himself published a challenging book defending his view of history.[27] But after his second exhibition at the Museum of Modern Art, it was clear that he had outstayed his welcome, an impression reinforced by his more recent gallery shows.[28] Perhaps, however, some skilled curator will revive Stella's art, which certainly remains of great sociological interest.

Curators like Rubin have especial power when tastes are changing. After Abstract Expressionism, there was great interest in figuring out what would come next. Leon Golub, who was a very challenging painter, had some distinguished champions. But his last retrospective, very near the end of his long life, was at the Brooklyn Museum, and not in Manhattan.[29] He remains, then, still a relatively marginal figure. Jasper Johns came to attention at roughly the same moment as Golub. He has always had his critics, but by contrast, his status among the great artists of his generation seems relatively secure. The post-Abstract Expressionists championed by Greenberg and Michael Fried have failed to find more than a modest place in history. Anthony Caro, so highly praised in the 1960s, now inspires highly critical responses.[30] And not even the eloquent championship of John Elderfield has entirely saved Morris Louis.[31] The other painters Fried praised so highly, Kenneth Noland and Jules Olitski, now seem minor. But perhaps that will inspire some young curator to reevaluate their art. Some young abstract artists identify themselves as Olitski's followers, but as yet, they have not persuaded the art world to pay much attention to them.[32]

Revivals of taste sponsored by curators are often very interesting. The recent apotheosis of Gordon Matta-Clark and Robert Smithson is a fascinating demonstration of how dramatically taste can shift.[33] In the Abstract Expressionist era, Sam Francis was controversial. After making some great early works of art, he produced too many paintings and works on paper, some frankly bad. A poorly edited posthumous retrospective failed to provide a convincing revisionist vision of his career.[34] Richard Diebenkorn, the other great California painter of Francis's generation, also has a relatively marginal place in the story of American art. But his recent retrospective was much more successful.[35] A show need not be large to have a significant effect, as two highly successful exhibits at C&M Arts in Manhattan in 2002 demonstrated. Ed Ruscha's *Birds, Fish and Offspring* introduced a significant small group of paintings to the larger public.[36] And *Jeff Koons: Highlights of 25 Years* showed that Koons is a figure to reckon with.[37]

Great curators must take risks. An exhibit of Matisse's art circa 1910, like a Poussin retrospective, is wonderful, but uncontroversial. As much as I enjoy seeing masterpieces, I often am more interested in challenging exhibitions that don't necessarily attract large audiences. A curator at a grand museum can relatively easily secure loans of masterpieces. By contrast, someone employed at a small museum or an alternative space must be more ingenious. That is why I have a special pleasure in great shows done by hole-in-the-wall galleries. Inspired by Holland Cotter's review in the *New York Times*, I went to an exhibition in 2004 at Gigantic Art Space, a small New York alternative space. I reviewed *Dtroit*, a show about art made in the city of

Detroit,[38] in which the curator Trevor Schoonmaker provided a revelatory portrait of art from a decaying city. And in 2005, I praised highly a show in a tiny Chelsea gallery by Charlotte Beckett, a former student of mine who is studying for her MFA at Hunter College.[39] But just as I approach a review of a book based upon a recent doctoral thesis done by a marginal scholar differently from one of a publication by a senior professor who occupies an endowed chair at Princeton, so I tend to be charitable about such exhibitions.

Minority artists seem especially difficult for curators to present in fair, uncondescending ways. Thaddeus Mosley, a senior African-American sculptor who lives and works in Pittsburgh, is a provincial figure who deserves credit for developing a significant body of art in a highly unsympathetic environment.[40] Charles "Teenie" Harris, a different case, was a great black Pittsburgh photographer who only recently has achieved the recognition he deserves.[41] Relatively marginal museums also have to work harder, as recently did the Brooklyn Museum when it showed Jean-Michel Basquiat. I loved this exhibition, which for me was revelatory.[42] And perhaps it was appropriate that a gifted African-American New Yorker was shown in his home borough. But had this show been in the Museum of Modern Art, I would have been more critical. One gallery that consistently puts on visually compelling displays is PaceWildenstein in New York. What most interests me is not the ability to display obvious masterpieces, but what these shows can do for problematic art. Just as a gifted editor can make writers seem more intelligent then we really are, so a very smart curator can make some merely good paintings look great.

Florence was the best place for painters, Vasari wrote in 1550, because artists there "must know how to make money, seeing that the territory...is not so wide or abundant as to enable her to support at little cost all who live there, as can be done in countries that are rich enough."[43] He offers a perfect description of New York today, for great art is created only in highly competitive environments. If you, a young curator, are offered a choice between being chief curator of contemporary art at a provincial institution—say, the Cleveland Museum of Art—or, rather, working for some hole in the wall in Brooklyn or on the sixth floor in Chelsea, do not hesitate for a moment. Take the New York job. There is a striking difference between the level of skill found in Manhattan curators (and critics) and those in the larger culture, at least once you get outside the more important museums. We provincial critics tend to not publicly discuss this situation, for doing so alienates our colleagues and neighbors. In New York there are so many collectors, critics, and curators that the stakes are high. If you are not extremely talented, you will not survive long. Everyone complains about the *New York Times*'s critics, but they all are polished professionals with challenging points of view. By contrast, most art writers in provincial cities like Cleveland, where I teach, or Pittsburgh, where I live, are amateurish journalists. These cities rarely produce good artists who stay in town, and their curators tend to be trained elsewhere. Reviewing frankly incompetent provincial exhibitions, like shooting fish in a barrel, soon becomes frankly dispiriting.[44]

Compared to present-day critics, Diderot and Baudelaire lived in what now seem very constricted art worlds. Notwithstanding all of their obvious practical problems, our curators are comparatively lucky. If I could wave a wand and change in just one way their practice, I would seek more accessible catalog essays. Nowadays these publications generally fall into two categories: Old-master shows present elaborate footnoted essays, experts debating before their graduate students. And displays of contemporary art employ inaccessible theorizing. Present-day academic art writing tends to be theory-bound, in ways that make it determinedly user-unfriendly. I admired greatly an exhibition of contemporary African Diaspora art in St. Louis in the fall of 2003.[45] But the fat catalog was frankly impenetrable. *3 x Abstraction: New Methods of Drawing by Emma Kunz, Hilma af Klint, and Agnes Martin*, at the Drawing Center, in New York, in 2005, was a revelatory exhibition. But the expensive, fully illustrated catalog presented very obscure, essentially irrelevant debates. If I, a tenured professor paid to teach smart students how to decipher these texts, find this writing frankly tedious, then what can the larger public make of it? Contemporary art needs to be made as accessible as possible. The publications of Arthur Danto are an important model, for his very serious writing is always lucid. He is the great philosopher of art of our day, and so his arguments should be taken seriously by aspiring curators. Danto curated a show at the Bergen Kunstmuseum in 1998, presenting in the catalog his theory of our post-historical era.[46] I hope that younger curators will read and emulate Danto's prose.

Writing as a critic, I would love that my commentaries matter. But when I study the recent history of the art world, then I realize that this hope is a delusion. Greenberg mattered for, as I have said, he had taste and a view of modernism, which became enormously influential. But since his day, things have changed. The writing of Danto, the only American critic who has equivalent intellectual prestige, does not have much effect on the art world. According to him, we live in a pluralistic era, which means that Robert Mangold, Sean Scully, Cindy Sherman, Mark Tansey and many other artists he admires co-exist. Unlike Greenberg, Danto does not offer an historical analysis or make judgments about taste which influence curators. And as for the rest of we art writers, our claims certainly do not have much effect on art world practice. Now it is the judgments of curators and collectors that influence what art is displayed, sold and admired. What the display of contemporary art became big business, this marginalization of critics became inevitable.

I have curated several provincial exhibitions, and one in New York.[47] In Pittsburgh, I worked with a local group, the Associated Artists of Pittsburgh, to present its annual show.[48] And in Cleveland, I co-curated an exhibition in collaboration with Cathleen Chaffee.[49] Art writers can learn a great deal by curating, if only because it inspires humility. Just as very few of the enormous number of contemporary works of art retain their interest for very long, so few shows have much staying power. Writing as a critic, I am aware of certain tensions between critics and curators. A positive review in the *New York Times* or the *Village Voice* can be a great help to a young artist or one of the smaller museums. But otherwise, compared with curators, most critics do not have much effect upon the art world. Everyone wants to be reviewed, but only rarely do museums cultivate critics. Regularly when I do reviews, some museums and galleries—the Whitney and the Gardner Museum in Boston, for example—refuse to provide catalogs. These institutions really ought to support critics, for our reviews provide essential publicity. Curators mostly are poorly paid, but critics of course make even less, which is why we support ourselves with day jobs.

I have tried to explain why curators matter to the larger public. But I should also mention, in conclusion, my personal reason for caring about their labors. In the 1980s I was making the transition from teaching philosophy to writing art criticism. Then I saw the exhibitions devoted to Manet, in 1983, and Caravaggio, in 1985, at the Metropolitan Museum of Art.[50] Bringing the paintings together made it natural to reflect upon Manet's and Caravaggio's stylistic development, the claims for their place in the canon, and the conflicting interpretations of their art. And the magnificent catalogs, with full bibliographies, made it easy to study the literature. Thanks to these exhibitions, I was inspired to become an art historian.

1. Alexander Nehamas, *Nietzsche. Life as Literature* (Cambridge, Massachusetts and London: Harvard University Press, 1985), p. 72.

2. See Clement Greenberg, *The Collected Essays and Criticism. Volume 4. Modernism with a Vengeance, 1957-1969* , Edited by John O'Brian (Chicago and London: University of Chicago Press, 1993), p. 324.

3. See my "Robert Rauschenberg: The Silkscreen Paintings, 1962-1964," *The Burlington Magazine*, March 1991, pp. 218-9.

4. See my "Michael Steiner," *Modern Painters*, July-August 2006, pp. 109-10.

5. My analysis draws upon the critical review by Margarita Tupitsyn, *Artforum*, November 2005, pp. 247, 289.

6. See my "Robert Ryman at Museum of Modern Art, New Art," *The Burlington Magazine*, December 1993, pp. 854-5.

7. See my "Alex Katz at PS 1," *The Burlington Magazine*, July 1998, pp. 504-6.

8. See my "Sylvain Laveissière. Pierre-Paul Prud'hon. The Metropolitan Museum of Art, New York." CAA Online reviews, October 1998.

9. See my "Morandi at the Guggenheim, Lichtenstein at the Whitney, Kitaj at the Hirshhorn," *Artscribe* 33, 1982, pp. 61-3.

10. See my "Ellsworth Kelly, Guggenheim Museum," *The Burlington Magazine*, January 1997. p. 68.

11. See my "Cai Gou-Qiang at Mass MoCA," *Artforum*, February 2005, pp. 176-7.

12. See my "Jim Hodges at MOCA," *Artforum*, April 2005, pp. 192-93.

13. I recall with amusement a Soho show in the 1980s, "Morandi and his Contemporaries." It showed one Morandi watercolor and some very modest paintings by other artists.

14. This, at any rate, seems the judgment of Warhol's recent commentators. I did not see this exhibition; see Robert Hughes, "The Rise of Andy Warhol," reprinted in *The Critical Response to Andy Warhol*, ed. Alan R. Pratt (Westport, Connecticut and London: Greenwood Press, 1997), pp. 146-58.

15. My review of first of these shows is "Picasso/Matisse. Fort Worth," *Modern Painters*, Summer 1999, pp. 92-93.

16. My review "Afterlight. Exhibiting Abstract Painting in the Era of Its Belatedness," *Arts,* March 1992, pp. 60-1, was too charitable.

17. This parallel is discussed in my *Writing About Visual Art* (New York: Allworth Press, 2003), Chapters 4 and 5.

18. See my "Made in California 1999-2000," LA County Museum of Art and Paul McCarthy, Museum of Contemporary Art, *The Burlington Magazine*, February 2001, pp. 122-23.

19. See my "Patti Smith, Warhol Museum, Pittsburgh," *Artforum*, December 2002, p. 142.

20. See my "Jean Cocteau, Andy Warhol Museum, Pittsburgh," *Artforum*, February 2001, p. 156.

21. A shrewd guide to art marketing is provided by Richard Polsky, who divides contemporary artists into three categories: buy, hold, and sell. See his http://www.artnet.com/Magazine/features/polsky.asp.

22. My *Artwriting* (Amherst: University of Massachusetts, l987) argues that Denis Diderot's Rameau's Nephew provides a very congenial description of this situation.

23. See my "Pittsburgh. 1985 Carnegie International," *The Burlington Magazine*, January 1986, p. 63; "Carnegie International," *Arts*, February 1992, p. 69; "New York. Whitney Biennial," *The Burlington Magazine*, June 1995, pp. 409-10; "Carnegie International," *Artforum*, January 1996, pp. 88-9; "New York, Whitney Biennial and other shows," *The Burlington Magazine*, May 1997, pp. 350-2; "1999 Carnegie International. Carnegie Museum of Art, Pittsburgh," *The Burlington Magazine*, February 2000, pp. 128-129; "New York. Whitney Biennial," *The Burlington Magazine*, June 2002, pp. 382-3.

24. See my *Sean Scully* (London: Thames and Hudson, 2004).

25. See my *Poussin's Paintings: A Study in Art-Historical Methodology* (University Park and London: Pennsylvania State University Press, 1993).

26. See their *Art Since 1900. Volume 2. 1945 to the Present* (New York: Thames & Hudson, 2004).

27. My response with David Reed was "Tradition, 'Ecclecticism' and Community. Baroque Art and Abstract Painting," *Arts*, January 1991, pp. 44-9. See also my "'Going for Baroque', Walters Art Gallery, Baltimore," *The Burlington Magazine*, January 1996, p. 59, a review of a show presenting Stella's claim that his abstract paintings are linked to baroque art.

28. See my "Frank Stella at Paul Kasmin Gallery," *tema celeste* 90, April 2002, p. 82.

29. See my "Leon Golub," *tema celeste*, September-October 2001, p. 82.

30. See my "New York, Recent Exhibitions," *The Burlington Magazine*, January 2003, p. 56-57.

31. See my "New York, Museum of Modern Art. Morris Louis 1912-1962," *The Burlington Magazine*, December 1986, pp. 926-7.

32. See my catalog essay "New New Painting and the History of American-Style Abstraction," *The New New Painters* (Flint Institute of Arts, 1999), pp. 9-11.

33. See Thomas Crow, *The Rise of the Sixties: American and European Art in the Era of Dissent* (New Haven:

Yale University Press, (revised edition) 2004).

34. See my "Sam Francis. Los Angeles," *The Burlington Magazine*, June 1999, pp. 382-3.

35. See my "Whitney. Richard Diebenkorn," *The Burlington Magazine*, December 1997, pp. 900-901.

36. Ed Ruscha, *Birds, Fish and Offspring* (C&M Arts, 2002).

37. Jeff Koons, *Highlight of 25 Years* (C&M Arts, 2004).

38. See my "Dtroit," *ArtUS* 3, June-August 2004, p. 43.

39. See my "Charlette Beckett," *ArtUS* 8, May-June 2005, p. 49.

40. See my "Thaddeus Mosley, Carnegie Museum of Art," *Artforum*, December 1997, p. 122.

41. See my "The Photographs of Charles 'Teenie' Harris, Westmoreland Museum of American Art," *Artforum*, May 2001, p. 180.

42. See my "Basquiat at the Brooklyn Museum," *ArtUS* 9, July-September 2005, p. 22-23.

43. Giorgio Vasari, *Lives of the Painters, Sculptors and Architects*, Translated by Gaston du C. de Vere (New York and Toronto: Everyman's Library, 1996), Volume 1, 584.

44. See, for example, my "Dan Tranberg, the Bonfoey Company," *Cleveland Plain-Dealer*, March 23, 2002, C4.

45. See my "A Fiction of Authenticity," Contemporary Art Center St. Louis, *Artforum*, March 2004, p. 188.

46. See his catalog essay *Bergen Kunstmuseum ved Arthur Danto* (Bergen, 1998).

47. My New York show, *Seven American Abstract Artists*, RuggerioHenis Gallery, New York, November 1988, was one of those group shows of abstract art I criticize earlier.

48. Associated Artists of Pittsburgh, Annual Exhibition, Carnegie Museum, Pittsburgh, August 2001. With catalog essay. See also my "New York Art, Pittsburgh Art, Art," *The Journal of Aesthetic Education*, 37, 3, Fall 2003, pp. 97-104.

49. With Cathleen Chaffee, *Wish You Were Here: The Art of Adventure*, (Cleveland: Cleveland Institute of Art, 2003), with my catalog essay, "Wish you were here: Artistic Adventures in Reality," pp. 9-13.

50. See my *Principles of Art History Writing* (University Park, Pennsylvania: Pennsylvania State University Press, 1991), Chapters 3 and 10.

I thank Cathleen Chaffee for reading a draft of this essay.

David Carrier is Champney Family Professor, a position divided between Case Western Reserve University and the Cleveland Institute of Art. He was been a Lecturer at Princeton University, a Getty Scholar, and a Clark Fellow. For 2006-2007 he is a Senior Fellow at the National Humanities Center. He has published books on the methodology of art history, Poussin's paintings, Baudelaire's art criticism, and the abstract artist Sean Scully. His most recent book is *Museum Skepticism* (Duke University Press). He has lectured extensively in the United States, China, India, and New Zealand. And he was published art criticism in *Artforum*, *ArtUS*, *The Burlington Magazine*, and *tema celeste*.

Dave Hickey

Beau Monde, Upon Reflection

Two years ago, I accepted Site Santa Fe's invitation to curate an international biennial exhibition in New Mexico. It would have been cowardly not to accept, I thought, after thirty years of taking issue with other curators' exhibitions. Also, I wanted to do it. Criticism and curating are radically distinct activities and I welcomed the change. Art critics toil on the consumer side of the art world, trying to make sense of what they are shown. Curators reign on the supply side, assembling works of art that other people might make sense of. As a longtime critic, I thought it would be fun, just once, to plan the party rather than reporting on the guest-list. I felt empowered to do so by the fact that exhibitions of serious art and critical essays about serious art do, in fact, have one thing in common: They are not themselves serious art. They are both highly conventionalized popular art forms. Like popular songs and residential architecture, art exhibitions are virtually identical in their parts, in their construction and manner of address. Critical essays are equally similar. One differs from another only in refinement and detail. Whatever profundity they might aspire to, they derive from the serious art they engage.

The audience for such works of popular art, then, has an experience that is only microscopically different from experiences he or she has had before. As a consequence, this audience, inured by the conventions of the genre, is predisposed to overlook the subtle arguments and theoretical superstructures that inform such work. What they *will* take away from the experience, invariably, is the *tone* of the performance—the ambient atmosphere conveyed by the accumulation of small decisions. With this in mind, I resolved at the outset to concern myself as a curator with refinement and detail—to *touch everything* with high spirits and a light heart—and let good art take care of the rest.

So, this is the way it went. I decided to call this exhibition *Beau Monde* for various reasons. First, because, many years ago, I wrote a book about beauty and have ever since been dubbed as the "beauty guy" by the popular press. It seemed best to beard this seedy lion in its den. Second, the show was scheduled to open on

Bastille Day, when the French celebrate the death of an antique *beau monde*. This seemed an appropriate birthday for a new *beau monde*. Finally, the expression *beau monde* refers literally to a beautiful world and figuratively to an elite social milieu. Like any good democrat, I wished to conflate these meanings and create a beautiful, non-exclusionary social milieu—a *beau monde* generally, rather than *le beau monde* specifically. Also, I wished to comment obliquely on the international art world, which, at present, is a *beau monde* not much concerned with the *beaux-arts*.

In truth, I didn't think about it. *Beau Monde* seemed a light hearted and high-spirited title. It felt right so I picked it and moved on to the next rats-nest of details. All of the preceding "becauses," in fact, are after the fact, as are most of the "becauses" that follow. They amount to a teleological unpacking of cumulative decisions made quickly, in sequence and on the spot. In practice, I tried to select good works of art from all of the artists I selected, and I selected ninety percent of these artists in five minutes on a Southwest Airlines flight from Las Vegas to Los Angeles, writing their names down on a yellow pad: my "dream team." The list was expressive of my own tastes, whims, intellectual concerns, tactical instincts, and art historical consciousness at the moment. These are now embodied in the exhibition, and, even though sorting one reason out from another is blatantly artificial and probably irrelevant, I have tried to do a little sorting in the paragraphs that follow, simply because nothing comes from nowhere.

I can see in retrospect, for instance, that I instinctively chose to do a self-consciously "art historical" exhibition because it's what I know, because international exhibitions are art historical occasions, and because most exhibitions of this sort are willfully disdainful of anything so parochial as art history. They aspire to a more totalizing "historical consciousness." As a practicing critic, I am congenitally skeptical of totalizing historical concepts, so I decided that in this exhibition I would momentarily abandon the quest for "truth" and strive for distinction—that I would, in short, try my very best not to be boring. Not being boring, thankfully, requires little in the way of totalizing historical consciousness, but it does require a modicum of art historical awareness.

Igor Stravinsky always argued that an artist without tradition is doomed to plagiarism, and what he meant by this, I think, is that, without some historical awareness, the precedents for what we do are indistinguishable from the art we practice. We know precedents whether we know that we know them or not, so unless we are acutely conscious of the accumulating tradition in which we work, unless we learn what we know, we plagiarize. Presented with the task of selecting an international exhibition in Santa Fe, New Mexico, I took Stravinski's cautionary observation to heart. I began asking myself how, specifically, my own exhibition would distinguish itself from other international biennials, and how, specifically, my exhibition would distinguish itself from its site in Santa Fe, New Mexico. My answer to each of these questions turned out to be the same answer: I would privilege the cosmopolitan.

Over the years, international biennials have become quintessential cosmopolitan occasions perversely devoted to marketing ideas of regional identity and local exceptionality in the normative global language of post-minimalist artistic practice. Over a somewhat longer period, Santa Fe has evolved into a quintessential cosmopolitan vacation community that is also devoted to marketing fantasies of local exceptionality in the international idiom of resort iconography. Both of these historical traditions presume that one place differs from another in its essence—in its essential content and circumstances—and that this essence can be communicated in an international language.

My quarrel with these rationales is twofold. First, the idea of global society as a collection of virtually autonomous provincial enclaves seems fantastical on its face. Second, the idea that the autonomous content of these provincial enclaves might be communicated in a single international idiom seems equally fantastical, and contradictory to the first idea—positing, as it does, some Platonic, international community of "understanding." The cautionary historical residue of this second proposition—the idea of a "global style"—was demonstrated for me in Robert Rosenblum's shrewd and elegant exhibition, *1900*, which opened at the Guggenheim Museum in New York in 2000. In *1900*, Rosenblum surveyed the last previous moment of international stylistic hegemony—at the turn of the 20th century, when post-impressionism rather than post-minimalism was the dominant idiom.

What Rosenblum's exhibition made legible, at least to me, was the extent to which externally imposed styles deaden practice. On the walls of the Guggenheim, the crippling artifice of by-the-book Japanese and Scandinavian post-impressionism contrasted radically with French post-impressionism that freely appropriated from Japanese and Northern European sources. The lesson of this (which, of course, we already know) is that it is always safest to assume that places differ from one another not so much in the things that are done as in the way things are done. Style, then, is, irrevocably, cultural content. As a curator, accepting this precept requires adopting a cosmopolitan rather than a global model of art practice. One must presume that, like politics and economics, all aesthetics are local, competitive, and impure—that art created in and for local venues acquires cosmopolitan attributes for local competitive advantage. This has been the case, I think, since Dürer went to Italy to become a better German artist, since Bassano cribbed the Germans for leverage in Venice, and, even today, outside the stylistic hegemony of institutional culture, it continues to be the case. In a cosmopolitan world of contiguous neighborhoods with porous boundaries, those neighborhoods whose artists and tradesmen most readily appropriate and adapt exotic attributes tend to predominate.

To take the case in point, the very richness of Santa Fe as a place derives from a stunning variety of cosmopolitan accommodations. Nothing, in fact, could be more eccentrically cosmopolitan than the area's porous and accommodating "spiritual climate," which allows the city of Santa Fe to function peacefully as a kind of transcendental souk in which Catholics, Navajos, Buddhists, Zunis, Baptists, Jews, Sikhs, Vegans, and nuclear physicists vie for competitive spiritual advantage. "Santa Fe Style" itself derives from an unstable blend of romantic primitivism, native design, international-style modernism, and Hacienda Victorian décor. The same conditions have prevailed in the great art centers of the late 20th century. Far from manifesting autonomous integrity, the art produced in New York, Cologne, Tokyo, London, and Los Angeles during this period is defined by its acquisitive impurity. One may, of course, disapprove of this mongrelization on the grounds that it simultaneously subverts the autonomy of place, the autonomy of culture, and the autonomy of the artist. The hypocrisies inherent in espousing an internationally administered global provincialism, however, argue against doing so.

Through this thought process (much slowed down and gentrified by my description of it), it became obvious to me that I could honor my own interests and the tradition of international exhibitions (while distinguishing my exhibition from both its predecessors and its site) by simply emphasizing the suppressed *cosmopolitan* aspect of an international exhibition in the city of Santa Fe. I could do this by prioritizing the impurity and complexity of both the occasion and the city rather than focusing on their separate, utopian aspirations to simplicity and purity. With this in mind, I set out to select works of art that visibly expressed the influence and confluence of diverse cultural resources. In the process, two operating strategies presented themselves. First, rather than asking the post-minimalist question, "How rough can it get and still remain meaningful?" I found myself asking the cosmopolitan question: "How smooth can it get and still resist rationalization?" This, because, in a post-industrial world in which everything is presumed to be temporary, nothing need *look* temporary, nor look the same. Secondly, in order to maintain a substrata of coherence while still privileging exuberance, I found myself selecting works that complemented one another as colors do, pairing works that define a category of practice while sharing no attributes beyond those that define the category. Gradually, the works began arranging themselves in larger constellations of concern.

Thus, I had no sooner embarked upon the purportedly earnest activity of curating, haphazardly creating networks of visual confluence and cross-reference, than it became clear to me that, by distinguishing my exhibition from the biennial tradition, I was also expanding its traditional mandate. Biennial exhibitions have always been designed to privilege the regional, ethnic and gender diversity of the artists exhibited. They have been so successful in doing this, in fact, that, in the present moment, one can hardly do otherwise. Such exhibitions, however, have also tended to privilege art made in the dominant post-minimal style by artists of a single, mid-career generation. In the process of solving my cosmopolitan acrostic, proceeding through the field logic of complements and constellations, I found myself expanding this narrow generational aperture, selecting work by artists spanning a half-century of contemporary art history—revealing, in the process, a host of cross-generational influences and affinities.

Moreover, having opened my field of selection to a multiplicity of cultural influences, I found that radical stylistic diversity was virtually unavoidable. Somehow, it seemed, modernist, post-minimalist, and post-conceptual styles of various flavors and aromas were going to co-exist in the space, and share that space with artists' works whose penchant for cosmopolitan sociability and historical stylistic development mirrors high art practice. Traditionally, international exhibitions that celebrate myths of cultural autonomy have included "outsider" art whose creators may be considered absolutely autonomous—who, in Peter Schjeldahl's phrase, constitute a "culture of one." By privileging the cosmopolitan, I gained access to an entirely different field of "outsider" practice, which, since it is no more outside than anything else in the exhibition, fit seamlessly into the ambient chaos.

Amazingly enough, I had the foresight to expect the ambient chaos, simply on account of my catholic tastes. Thus, I decided early on to accommodate SITE Santa Fe's building to the art rather than asking the artists to accommodate their work to the local site, as is usually done. My first act, in fact, when I was contacted about the possibility of curating this exhibition was to contact Graft Design and solicit their complicity. My idea from the first, and Graft's as well, was to make a space that would make a place for everything—to design a melting pot in which nothing melts. Our general strategy was to invent a space with rich historical precedents that was invested with a sense of occasion. Ultimately, we created a building that is part Italian palazzo and part informal garden. As a palazzo, the *Beau Monde* building has a formal approach, a façade, an entry hall, a grand hall, and a chapel; it has a mirrored ball-room salon, an elevated petit salon, a grand salon, and three withdrawing rooms. As a garden, it is patterned as a flow-through, peripatetic space with a grand vista that extends from the entrance, diagonally through the space, and out a new window in the back of the building; it has various tantalizing invitations in the form of glimpses and glowing doorways, and an unfolding sequence of visible destinations.

Thus the actual positioning of the works of art had less to do with arranging objects than with choreographing the ideal viewing territories each work demanded. Some of the works in the exhibition were designed to be walked by; some of the work was designed to be walked through, and these were given their transits. Some works were best to be among and were given their discrete spaces. Most of the works of art in the exhibition, however, were designed to be approached from a distance, thus a great deal of the design work went into making these works directly approachable; the rest went into making the whole space work together and to complicating this subliminal smoothness by investing each space with its own fictional ambience. For whatever it's worth, we were able to do this to our own satisfaction, and virtually no design work was done on site. A few features were added, a few subtracted, but, basically, we built in Santa Fe what we designed in Los Angeles.

What I had not foreseen was the extent to which shifting the emphasis of the exhibition toward the cosmopolitan and directing its tone toward the high-spirited and light hearted would influence the "look" of the show. It soon became apparent, however, that the high-spirited accommodation of disparate cultural influences in works of art expresses itself, in practice, as a series of bravura solutions to problems of arrangement and articulation. Exhibitions that aspire to communicate the psycho-logical circumstances of cultural identity, I realized, tend to be composed of art that states problems. The art in *Beau Monde* aspired to solve problems, on the assumption that the visible resolution of cultural dissonance has its moral and intellectual conse-quences, its social allegories, its uses and functions.

Looking at the work after it was selected and before it was installed, I discovered further that, in works of art, successful cross-cultural engagement (or cultural impurity, if you will) manifests itself in two distinct ways. The confluent cultures either express themselves in the inclusive, intricate complexity of *bricolage* or in the simplicity of abstract structures arising at generalized points of cultural intersection. Cosmopolitan art, I quickly realized, is, almost of necessity, either simpler or more complex than monocultural production. This, I think, accounts for the unusual division of works in the exhibition between abstract simplicity and ebullient complexity.

The aspect of cosmopolitan art that I probably understood beforehand, but had never successfully articulated, is that, in its radical simplicity and ebullient complexity, it tends to privilege the interpretive penchant of the beholder over his or her internalized cultural presumptions. This, in turn, tends to privilege the radical sociability of the work in congress and *in situ*. As a consequence, if you ask me what the assembly and display of all this art in a redesigned space in Santa Fe, New Mexico, might mean, I can only guess. My artist friend, Edward Ruscha, who is represented in this exhibition, once remarked to me that since both he and I beheld his finished work at about the same time, we both had an equal shot at guessing what it might mean. This is even more the case with an exhibition, since the curator's job is not to create meaning or to impose meaning on works of art, but to create the circumstances out of which meaning might arise—circumstances that might prove meaningful to the beholder. Finally, all I can offer is my own assurance that the exhibition, at its best, resembles my idea of a "beautiful world." If it is not your idea of a beautiful world, I can only hope that the exhibition articulates options and strategies out of which other beautiful worlds might be created.

Reprinted with permission of SITE Santa Fe. This essay was first published in *Beau Monde: Toward a Redeemed Cosmopolitanism*, the catalog accompanying SITE Santa Fe's Fourth International Biennial exhibition of the same title, curated by Dave Hickey (July 14, 2001 – January 6, 2002). Artists in the exhibition included: Kenneth Anger, Jo Baer, Jeff Burton, James Lee Byars, Pia Fries, Gajin Fujita, Graft Design, Frederick Hammersley, Marine Hugonnier, Jim Isermann, Ellsworth Kelly, Josiah McElheny, Darryl Montana, Sarah Morris, Takashi Murakami, Nic Nicosia, Kermit Oliver, Jorge Pardo, Ken Price, Stephen Prina, Bridget Riley, Ed Ruscha, Alexis Smith, Jesús Rafael Soto, Jennifer Steinkamp & Jimmy Johnson, Jessica Stockholder, Jane & Louise Wilson.

Re-reading this essay, I am delighted to find it dated. The institutional fashions with which I take issue in the essay are pretty much defunct today, having been replaced by indiscriminate fashion-mongering. Identity politics has morphed effortlessly into global niche marketing, instituting a whole new regime of intellectual vulgarity. I am, however, happy to have done *Beau Monde*. The public and my critical colleagues liked it. The professional biennial bureaucracy was not enchanted, but I liked it myself. It was a good place to be. There was a fifty foot square white room in the exhibition with gray wool carpet in which four large ceramic sculptures by Ken Price faced off with a four canvas ensemble by Ellsworth Kelly (now at the Beyler). That room was the best thing I have ever done, thanks to Ellsworth and Ken. It was exquisite and un-photographable. Even today, people come up to me and say, "Wow, you did that room!" As a curator, that's what pretty much what you want.

D.H. 8/06

Dave Hickey is a free-lance writer of fiction and cultural criticism. He has served as owner-director of A Clean Well-Lighted Place gallery in Austin, Texas, as director of the Reese Palley Gallery in New York City, as Executive Editor of *Art in America* Magazine, and as Contributing Editor to *The Village Voice*. He has written for most major American cultural publications including *The Rolling Stone*, *Art News*, *Art in America*, *Artforum*, *Interview*, *Harper's Magazine*, *Vanity Fair*, *Nest*, *The New York Times*, and *The Los Angeles Times*. His critical essays on art have been collected in two volumes: *The Invisible Dragon: Four Essays on Beauty* (Art Issues Press, 1993) and *Air Guitar, Essays on Art and Democracy* (Art Issues Press, 1998).

Sara Arrhenius

Independent Curating Within Institutions Without Walls

The first meeting took place in an austere and, for a Swedish art institution, surprisingly official office. Present are representatives of Göteborg's three art institutions: Göteborg Museum of Art, Göteborgs Konsthall, and the Hasselblad Center. They are hosting the Art Biennial, which was started up in the city four years ago; I was invited in as curator for the exhibition due to be launched in September 2005. We are now to meet for the first time to discuss the inevitable underpinnings of all exhibition-making: the institutional framework, the budget, fundraising, staff, marketing. This is, after all, a collaboration among the three institutions as much as between them and me; fields of play have to be marked out, roles and rules laid down, before the game can begin. Göteborg is Sweden's biggest west-coast city and the second-largest nationally, with a university, a school of fine arts and a series of cultural institutions with national standing, including the opera, the city theatre and the museums. The city's self-awareness has, among other things, generated a vigorous experimental music scene, with offshoots into sound art. But there are also strains of the provincialism intrinsic to the second city in a very small country.

For all its ordinariness, this meeting came to feel like a point of intersection for a number of the questions that inescapably arise when an external curator is invited to put on an event of this type and scale: How will the relationship between the local and the international be negotiated and played out? What possibilities are there for inscribing criticality into a high-profile art event, with its inherent logic of seeking maximum funding, audience numbers and media visibility? And what kind of relationship will be set up between the host institution and the guest curator—what explicit and implicit rules of conduct operate here, and how do they limit curatorial room to maneuver?

These questions also indirectly engage with a more general critical discussion of the current conditions surrounding exhibition curation. They speak to and about the new paradigm in cultural politics in Scandinavia, created by changes in the organization of cultural affairs in Scandinavia over the last decades. The regional model for the funding of culture and the arts is obviously a product of the Scandinavian welfare state; since the 1960s strong state and regional support for the arts has been the dominant funding structure. Both art institutions and individual artist production are mainly funded by state and regional support directed to the cultural producers through various grant systems. Given a small art market, a weak tradition in corporate sponsorship, and a lack of large, independent cultural foundations offering support for the arts, the policies developed by these funding bodies have had a substantial influence on cultural activities at large. The last decade has brought changes in the policies of these funding systems and in national and international cultural politics, as well as a reformulation of the prospects for and aims of cultural policy as a whole. The shift is very notable in Scandinavia, where the long tradition of vigorous national cultural support for the arts and strong national institutions is slowly being challenged by internationalization and new ways of organizing support for and the distribution and making of culture. This presents cultural producers with practical questions in daily practice, but on a more general level it also suggests more fundamental questions about the relationship between the curator, the institution and the funding organizations.

Among the products and symptoms of this development in cultural politics—a tendency that I think runs right through the global art system, though my viewpoint here is focused on the Scandinavian context—are the biennial in its current form, independent curators, and the new, expanding system for training curators. Using my specific work with the Biennial in Göteborg as a starting point, I will move on to a more general discussion of how the biennial as an exhibition format, a telling touchstone in considering the role of curatorial training programs in contemporary exhibition making, is predicated on this cultural-political change.

Dominating much of the critical writing on curating, the biennial has without doubt become a paradigmatic exhibition format. One could without hesitation call it a new form of institution, a museum without walls traveling the world with its own court treasurer, benefactor, and master of ceremonies, and played out in an increasingly globalized art scene. Recent years have seen biennials, festivals, and other recurring major art events spread like dandelion seeds—every country, region, and city has to have its own. Art has quite openly become part of a culture-and-entertainment industry, which in these days of structural rationalization is to replace the heavy industry that has been downsized and outsourced to another part of the world. Culture has somewhat surprisingly been given a job to do: it is a medicine for treating permanent unemployment and depopulation. It has been charged with creating identity and attracting skilled labor to regions of population flight, with uplifting rather dull small towns that can then be given a further facelift by espresso bars, restaurants, and shopping centers filled with identical chain shops selling clothes and furnishings.

In Scandinavia there is also a strong tendency to allow contemporary art to act as a kind of marker for the contemporary in other cultural or social contexts, such as historical museums or, in quite different settings, shopping centers, new buildings, and schools. Even if this way of working allows for a broadening of the audience and mode of address for art, one can see that contemporary art and the curator are playing a new and not uncomplicated role. Art gets to act as a kind of mediator of the contemporary that has to comment on a context, like a historical anthropological collection or a social situation outside the art institution, like an urban area in need of development. This practice represents a shift in the role of contemporary art that is of greater importance than one might at first imagine. Without its own historical context and institutional framework, contemporary art and its audience is left quite alone. This popular curatorial method in many ways brings the complex role of the independent curator into focus. Instead of being a specialist within a field of cultural science, such as contemporary or modern art, or perhaps even in a special genre, such as painting or drawing, the contemporary curator is a mediator of the contemporary, who both sets in motion and creates situations that frame and comment on the contemporary world in a broader field than just that of art. That this is a role with potential is something all can agree on. At the same time, I believe it is extremely important to visualize and discuss the new situations and negotiations to which this development gives rise. Such a discussion is necessary if the curator—and for that matter art—is not to become a kind of hostage to culture and to local-political strategies for development.

This shift of the role of art in contemporary society is having a tangible effect on the conditions which the independent curator has to work, but also on how educational courses for curators are being conceived and set up. One could say that the freelancing independent curator's role has developed in parallel with the rise of an ever more copious supply of temporary art projects—projects that do not necessarily have ties to national or local institutions, or that have only temporary links with them. The institutional framework that was previously dominant, at least when more alternative structures outside national or local institutions were not involved, has been replaced by a new, less visible structure. For what we are seeing in the Nordic region is the visual arts existing in increasingly direct, close interaction with a number of funding organizations and social institutions without the mediation of the art institution. If in the Scandinavian sphere the expectation from the public commissioning body was hitherto to reach out with art to as broad a public as possible with an educational aim in mind, then culture today has also taken on an identity-creating role—one that is politically useful, whether in employment policy, infrastructure, cultural geography, or social policy. This applies not least to the type of activity that is nowadays called "nation, city or region branding," in which countries and regions compete for visibility and appeal, with culture as just one instrument among others. This represents a shift both in art's place and in its room to maneuver, and the curator, independent or not, will encounter it in one way or another and have to work with or against it.

If the playing field of art has been enlarged, then at the same time it has become less distinct and been co-opted into an increasingly sophisticated and opaque network of regional, national and international exchanges and support systems, in which public and private funding and international, national, and regional organizations are closely intertwined. And, since new activities beget their own organizers and administrators, this system goes hand in hand with the development of an increasingly ramified and professionalized corps of curators, cultural producers, marketers, cultural administrators and fundraisers. Event-oriented cultural production that is generated just outside or in some sort of collaboration with established cultural institutions has created its own world of professions and career trajectories, a development that has also led to new educational courses for curators, cultural producers, and cultural administrators, a relatively new phenomenon in Scandinavia that is undergoing vigorous growth.

Curatorial training programs are an interesting indicator of our time in the sense that, unlike traditional higher education in fine arts, they are not directed at providing specialized knowledge within an academic field that is to be implemented at an institution with quite definite limits, traditions, and objectives. Instead, courses are given to people from highly diverse backgrounds—art, cultural history, journalism, marketing—so that they become a species of mediator of the contemporary, and of the cultural products that the contemporary world produces. Often, part of these courses' identity is that those taking them will in most cases work specifically as unattached cultural producers, what we call independent curators—a term that has quite a vague meaning and usage. The word "independent" seems in most cases to refer to working outside institutions in a quite concrete sense. At the same time, the term also seems to carry an aura of freedom, referring to a lack of ties, and to the possibility of acting without the influence of power relations, traditions, and pressures. But even with all the attraction implicit in the word, we have to admit that in many ways it obscures the conditions underlying the work of most independent curators. Most autonomous art projects rely on their curators' capacity for localization and for tying together the various funding options that exist for art and culture projects today. In actual fact, most independent art projects are a result of collaborations with various types of institutions: national organizations for promoting art and culture, corporate supported cultural foundations, international organizations for promoting cultural exchange. All these institutions have their more or less explicit agendas. But the boundaries of these organizations are more flexible and harder to define than the traditional art institution, the museum or the kunsthalle. Given the structural changes in the art system, new organizations that fall outside the reach of established curatorial theory and institutional critique have become influential but quite invisible actors.

Drawing on my own experience in building up the Swedish institution for international exchanges for Swedish artists, International Artists' Studio Program in Sweden (IASPIS), I would like to use these new, nationally based but internationally active organizations for supporting artists from a given region as an indicative example of this structural change in Scandinavian cultural politics. These institutions could be described as flexible support-and-lobbying institutions that operate both nationally and internationally. They are not exhibition producers in the traditional sense, and their impact and agenda are therefore harder to discern, let alone argue with. Instead they are subsumed into the infrastructure of art production via grants, support for productions, opinion formation, and research trips for curators and artists. The chances of getting support for exhibiting and producing the work of certain artists, and the discursive activity in the form of, for example, publications, seminars, and conferences, in a more elusive way, affect what is offered by the large biennials and how they are put together, along with artists' access to the international arena.

Together with the expanding biennials and other temporary art projects, these new organizations that support artists and exhibitions on a national and international basis form a new kind of institutional network. They have no visible walls, and with their short history, they are more flexible than the traditional institutions. This invisibility and mobility have obvious advantages, but they also make it harder to focus on and visualize the hidden agendas, the implicit power structures, and the logic of inclusion and exclusion that are also, unconsciously or not, a part of the anatomy of these organizations. Institutional critique is a staple of contemporary curatorial theory these days, and part of the routine of curatorial training programs. But the mechanisms of these new, invisible institutions without walls are still not discussed sufficiently within this process, which is mostly directed toward the traditional objects of institutional critique: the museum and the art market. Today's curatorial training programs are very good at teaching their students to master these new institutions—fundraising, project management, networking; curators are taught to be skilled actors in the new field of cultural production. But what is often left out of these programs is critical thinking about the field in which independent curating is operating. The changing structure of the art system demands a critical authority that will look more carefully at this cultural-political development and the new institutions it is generating, and incorporate this thinking into contemporary curatorial training and practice.

In this essay I have been trying to show how difficult it is to define independent curating in opposition to institutional curating and to think of these two positions in terms of working "inside" or "outside" the institution. I've been trying to relate the blurred boundaries between independent and institutional curating to a structural change in the cultural landscape where new organizations for culture production is developing within which curators have to operate. This new institutional topography changes the way we have up to now defined the art institution and terms such as "independent" and "institutional." This new situation makes it urgent to develop a critical theory and practice that incorporates this cultural-political development, and to analyze it so as to develop new curatorial tools. One natural platform for this body of thinking would be within the curatorial training programs themselves, which could become active agents in this process. To establish the possibility of such theory production, I see it as vital that the training programs not only consist of shorter, more instrumentally oriented courses, but also that they are set up as theory producing research institutions. We need to develop tools not only for managing this culture, but also for critical thought about the political agendas underlying the current situation, for making visible the new structures of cultural institutions that are organizing the art system, and for making this thinking a part of curatorial practice.

A few months into our work on the Biennial in Göteborg, a decision was made to hold a meeting with the city's politicians. A special group had been appointed that was to monitor the work on the Biennial. It was emphasized that there was no intention of influencing the artistic running or of directing the work in any way; the purpose was informative, so as to be able to prepare for any reactions from the public. But the somewhat unclear role and identity that characterizes the visiting curator's position was never so evident in the work on the Biennial as at that moment. In Scandinavia, the cultural-political development discussed above has minimized the distance between cultural producers and funding bodies run by politicians over the last decade. Temporary projects are often initiated without negotiating a production structure that guarantees artistic freedom to the curator. In such projects, responsibility is hard to pin down, as it floats between the institution, the funding system, and the invited guest curator. As an outsider, a guest curator does not know a lot about the discussions that have preceded such meetings and against what background one is acting. How are the contacts between the art institutions and politicians set up in a small city like this? What freedom does one have with regard to the commissioning body, and how does one justify the support one receives in the face of competition from other activities? The question of where these issues should be raised, discussed and negotiated is seldom an explicit part of the curatorial process; the economic and institutional backbones of an art exhibition are usually only visible in the obligatory credit lines. One possible way to strengthen the artistic independence of the curator would be to make negotiations with funding structures and the different institutions involved in realizing projects a transparent part of the curatorial process.

Within the framework of the traditional Scandinavian model for cultural politics, the institutions' relationship with political structures is formulated as part of a permanent institutional organization, one devised and recognized in the implementation of a general policy on culture affairs. For a temporary art event that moves among different local communities, political landscapes, and funding structures, these criteria must be negotiated anew every time, in a constantly changing topography of exhibitions, biennials, and art fairs. In this situation, I think it is more crucial than ever for independent curators not to entertain a self-image of being innocently independent, but to think of themselves as active agents within a framework, in which questions of curatorial freedom, the role of funding organizations, culture-political agendas, and the ideology of the participating organizations are to be discussed and analyzed as part of the work.

Funding organizations and political structures wanting to monitor and interfere in cultural activities is not a new phenomenon. But I do think that the presence of the group of politicians in the Biennial office can be read as a symptom of a shift in the understanding of the limits of freedom of expression, and that this is linked with a change in the way the overall aim of support for cultural activities is defined in cultural policy in the Scandinavian sphere. Discussions of the limits of freedom of expression usually attribute it to a growing conservatism or to sensation-seeking art, depending on which side of the barricades one is standing on. And this model certainly has some explanatory power. But I think it is also valid to associate this shift with the changes in the structure of cultural politics. At a time when culture has become an instrumental tool for giving a certain city visibility, or for developing a region, the role of art is changing. By extension, I believe that the shift in the way we understand and use freedom of expression within cultural institutions will also come to alter the image of such institutions as an arena in which various notions and assertions are set off against one another, discussed, contradicted and analyzed. The concept of freedom of expression is not a static one; rather, it is in constant transformation and negotiation with its own time. Reading these transformations from a historical perspective is, of course, an indispensable part of curatorial training. But the independent curator also needs to take an active part in negotiating the definitions and boundaries of these issues within culture and in society at large, and to make it a part of daily curatorial practice.

I am sitting on a fast train between Stockholm and Göteborg, together with other weekly commuters. It strikes me how well the independent curator/cultural producer/artist fits into the image of the perfect workforce in the new Europe. Ten years ago, the independent curator seemed to belong to an alternative scene by choice. To work outside the institution offered possibilities of developing new strategies for curating and of offering an alternative to the dominant mode of exhibiting art. Today the independent curator's situation could be interpreted as a symptom of a more profound change in the working conditions of people working in the arts. The independent curator of today is mobile, willing to change, project-oriented, unattached to any specific place or institution. All of these characteristics carry a positive charge in the contemporary world and represent innovation and dynamism. It is precisely for that reason that it is appropriate to risk twisting and turning this image a bit. When one is always on the way to the next place and exhibition, one establishes a different relationship with a place and a public than when one has a more long-term involvement with an institutional framework. To question and develop an institution's structures and ways of working is not a part of the visiting curator's duties. That the playing field for the independent, freelance curator has become larger in recent years goes hand in hand with a dismantling of the institutions, with temporary projects coming to replace the work of a large permanent staff.

It is also interesting to try to uncover the concealed meanings that give the charge to the institutional/independent dichotomy in art and the world of culture. The institution usually stands for continuity and tradition, but also for inflexibility and traditionalism. The independent curator usually gets to represent innovation and the contemporary. The question is: What do we have to gain by charging up this dichotomy, and are these boundaries really so razor-sharp? There are a number of possibilities inherent in the new extended field for art and culture. But at the same time, one must be conscious of the covert or overt agendas that are built into these situations, and courses for curators should provide students with tools for dealing with the current political reality, in which these questions are ultimately negotiated.

Sara Arrhenius is a curator and writer. She is the director of Bonniers Konsthall, a new kunsthalle in Stockholm that opened in September 2006. She was the director of IASPIS (International Artists' Studio Program in Sweden) from 2001 to 2004. She was the curator of the third edition of Göteborg International Biennial for Contemporary Art, 2005. She has been an editor of the art magazine *Index* and a founding editor of *NU: The Nordic Art Review*. Arrhenius has served as a critic at the Swedish daily newspaper *Dagens Nyheter*, among other publications, and is a regular contributor to international and Swedish art magazines. She has published and edited several books, among them *Black Box Illuminated*, an anthology on the moving image in contemporary art, and *In Dialogue with Annika von Hausswolff*, both published by Propexus.

Young Chul Lee

Curating in a Global Age

Following the collapse of the Soviet Union, the world is experiencing a major cultural shift, with art activities showing a continual process of change within the global-local matrix while revealing cultural differences and plurality. In order to make them significant in the global age, the production of new localities resembles almost a kind of survival game, the activities of artists and curators from different locations forming a daily-changing global scene. This process internally challenges and alters the established definition and boundary of art itself, because it tends to be multi-disciplinary, trans-cultural, and an intervention of visual art that makes a new relationship between the private and public sphere. Considering overall transitional changes in the established definition and boundary of art, I attempt to address several points in regard to the problematic of exhibition making from critical perspectives and the changing role of the curator based on personal experiences and thoughts as an independent curator over the last ten years.

As an independent curator

As an independent curator, my experience and knowledge has not been outlined through art academy and curatorial studies. There were no curatorial programs until the mid-1990s and there are still no adequate programs in or outside the academic art system in Korea. This perhaps reflects the situation in other Asian countries. I studied sociology and aesthetics in the mid-1980s, when the anti-autocratic, anti-capitalist and the South and North Korea unification movements were intense. From 1989 to 1993, we formed an art criticism study group, studying various disciplines such as media study, literary theory, art criticism and theory, commodity aesthetics, and institution analysis in terms of Marxism and Poststructuralism. We had regular lengthy meetings among thirty or so young members. This experience was considered much more important than the academic system for young students during the 1980s, a period of drastic student and labor-led movements, when streets and universities were swamped with police-fired teargas. These autodidactic communities often operated in ways that were in marked contrast—hence in a way "counter" to—class-based and hierarchical communities. These study groups were likewise distinguished by their promotion of non-hierarchical, non-instrumentalized, or peer-to-peer learning, while at the same time they engaged in broader issues concerning knowledge production, ownership, and circulation. At the time, these progressive artists and critics, who prepared themselves for a fight with the "leviathan in sheep's clothing" (or market ideology), had to review their suppositions, alternatives, and strategies in order to speak to the current times and effect change. Rather than seeing culture as a total system, they conceived of it as a battleground for active arguments, or as a locus for various praxes and resistances. The progressive art movement, armed with more sophisticated politico-cultural strategies, had to embrace all the implications that were preciously rejected and to show flexibility in adjusting itself to the new situation it confronted.

The 2nd Gwangju Biennale offered the chance for these kinds of issues and questions to be raised and addressed. When I was working on the Biennale in 1997 (which included working with architects, photographers, and visual artists), my interest was to explore the comprehensive relationship found between a conceptual diagram and visual art from Deleuzean and poststructuralist perspectives. The primary goal of this exploration was to dissolve the confrontational relationship between the progressive theories of first world and the cultural politics of third world. Despite the fact that these progressive theories have legitimacy in anti-modernism movements, it was not clear whether so-called post-modern theories would be capable of contributing political resistance against eurocentricism or if they were just another reflection of hegemony of the west. These issues were put on the table during a symposium in which the participants expressed various viewpoints, including the opinion that the unified categories of nation, class, sex, culture, and languages should be rearticulated in the indeterminate, hybrid, interstitial, and negotiated space. This biennale, which attempted to link several topics in cultural studies after the 1980s and contemporary works of art, explored a way to deconstruct a hierarchical dualism that strengthened the regime of modernization. I proposed five themes to the participating curators: speed/water, space/fire, power/metal, hybrid/wood, becoming/earth, under the title Unmapping the Earth. The five curators and I intended to make an unfamiliar pool, a huge visual machine of cultural differences in the global-local matrix. The thing that interested me, in making a complex exhibition, was how each curator defined his own space and how we compose "inter space"— the cutting edge of translation and negotiation among different cultures.

Curatorial Space

Today, curatorial space appears to form the situational and/or ideological battle-ground for visual practices, which is in turn related to how this space is produced and reproduced through social praxis and processes. In Henri Lefebvre's *The Production of Space*, the author draws an important and, moreover, still topical conclusion on how space is articulated in western culture: "Space is not a container without content, a Kantian *a priori*, or an abstract mathematical continuum independent of human subjectivity and agency."[1] In pre-modern space, things within it are assigned a place along a predominantly vertical axis. Modern space, on the contrary, is Euclidean, horizontal, infinitely extensible, and therefore, in principle, boundless. Now we understand that space is not politically a neutral container (or simply context) within which social activities take place. In regard to its use, rights, or intervention, space goes beyond treating the subordinates as passive recipients of "occupying." Curators observe and experience the plurality of space through contestation and negotiation in the curatorial process. Therefore, curatorial space is often called the situational, relational, contested, differential, interstitial and nomadic space. In the spirit of the Situationists, Deleuze designates in his *A Thousand Plateaus* the trajectory of the same space as a nomadic aesthetics: "It is a space of affects, more than of properties. It is haptic, rather than optical perception. It is intensive, rather than extensive. It is based on symptoms and evaluations, rather than measures and properties. ...its orientations, landmarks, and linkages are in continuous variation: it operates step by step."[2] Throughout the act of composing a space and exploring inter-relations within it, a space of affects can be brought to life, and a space becomes a real world, society, and experiment. The role of the curator does not lie in contemplating the mortality of values of art or in reflecting on history. In order to arouse becoming, he negotiates, communicates and arbitrates with various kinds of people, including politicians, city officials, businessmen, collectors, and urban planners. He attempts to find a way to construct his own set of values in the present tense. We have to challenge our conventional way of thinking and expand our practice beyond our comfort zones. As the Situationists emphasized, the achievement of an art exhibition implies going beyond the boundaries of art, bringing creativity and adventure into the critique and liberation of every aspect of life; and first of all into challenging the submissive conditioning that prevents people from creating their own adventures, suggesting there is no world waiting to be created and experimented. The curator proposes questions. Questions are invented, like anything else. Here, the art of constructing a problem is important; you invent a problem, a problem-position, before finding a solution. Such questioning attempts to be context-sensitive with a twist and, if necessary, going in and trying to turn things in another direction. Context-sensitivity is about acknowledging the character of something and at the same time being able to swing that character around somehow.[3] However, the act of questioning tends to direct us toward the future or toward the past. We are accustomed to considering history as a means of thinking. Despite the fact that curating takes its departure point from history and it is inevitably historicized, it is not historical. Drawing from James Joyce, who said "History is a nightmare from which I am trying to wake up," history isn't experimental, but is just a totality of negative conditions that enables experimenting with something beyond history. However, history acquires another dimension when it serves as a set of preconditions to articulate cultural difference or when it is recycled to be re-historicized from anti-institutional or anti-academic perspectives. For instance, since the 1960s, many curators organized a-historical exhibitions as a critique of modernism, and many biennales take their subject matter from this tradition. Exhibition making is about constructing the in-between space that carries the burden of the meaning of cultural difference in the present tense. To borrow Homi Bhabha's term, it is about creating a "Third Space."[4] Third Space therefore ensures that cultural signs are not fixed but can be appropriated and reread. It is where pseudo-cultural diversity can be ruptured and where only the "inter" space can exist.

Geographical vs. Historical

> We are living in a post-Utopian epoch of reformism that seeks change within what exists, instead of *changer la vie*. But many transformations are taking place in silence. Part of them came out of Lampedusan strategy from power establishments, aimed to change so that everything remains the same. Power today doesn't strive to confront diversity, but to control it.
> —Gerardo Mosquera[5]

Adding on the previous points, to me exhibition making is not about history as discourses, but about a continual process of deconstructing history and of articulating the forgotten, hidden, and excluded elements. An exhibition is becoming itself. "Becoming is born in History, and falls back into it, but is not of it. In itself it has neither beginning nor end but only a milieu. It is thus more geographical than historical."[6] Geography literally means the action of drawing (graphy) on the earth (geo). Locality which is marked by "now here" is another side of the coin of globalization marked by "nowhere." In 2004, The Walker Art Center in Minneapolis, MN, organized a thought-provoking exhibition, *How Latitudes Become Forms: Art in a Global Age*. This exhibition took an in-depth, multi-disciplinary look at how contemporary art and culture are defined and presented in the global context. It was also in homage to what Szeemann identified in 1969, not only in terms of what artists were doing but in terms of the methodology and the language of exhibitions. The exhibition title was taken from Harald Szeemann's *When Attitudes Become Form*, which reflected the major change in the west that took place in the late 1960s. In most cases, what is borrowed is the sign, and not the total meaning, from the standpoint of the user. Transmitting an idea, a model, or a spatial habit causes a message to transform, allowing it to be somewhat meaningful for receivers in their own context. *When Attitudes Become Form* was a very important exhibition that signaled the beginning of international exhibitions, but also the peak of Eurocentrism. The artists involved in *When Attitudes Become Form* were almost exclusively from the United States and Europe. This exhibition was seminal in that it highlighted shifts in practice that are still very active today, framed the way institutions and curators worked, and identified a very specific range of aesthetics. The neutrality of the white cube as we know it in terms of the museum and gallery space is closely linked to a history of European essentialism and universalism that goes back to the Enlightenment. Szeemann's practice and the artists he was bringing to the fore started to challenge that assumption of neutrality. There is, I hope, a continuation of that critique in the work we curators are doing today. Geographically, we are changing our own latitude, and looking at other latitudes. And we are also giving ourselves latitude with regards to the way the institution of curating functions. Paulo Herkenhoff, one of the curators of the exhibition was attracted to Szeemann's exhibition subtitle *Live in Your Head*. Looking at the way art practice has developed over the last ten years, Herkenhoff liked the idea of substituting "world" for "head": *Live in your world*. The world is increasingly entering artwork as subject and material and more and more artists are trying to address issues in our world in a responsible way. Focusing on the specificity of places and the singularity of artists and their practices, *How Latitudes Become Forms* disrupts the idea of curatorial practice as tourism, cultural shopping, or the researching of "token artists" for geopolitical purposes. The etymology and meaning of the word latitude is a transverse dimension: breadth, width as opposed to length, also occasionally spaciousness. Unlike the old Northern Hemispheric system of compiling "world surveys," which occasionally incorporated artists from Latin America or Africa as long as they lived in metropolitan cities, curating a show such as *How*

Latitudes Become Forms required actual traveling and personal engagement by the curators. It was not a geographic survey attempting to sum up such a multitude of "local places." Rather, it was a constellation comprising "localizations" of artistic practice developed by the individual experience of each curator. It presented not a homogenization but a poetical semblance of the parcours. If it aims for any "semblance of a whole," it is by understanding its own potentiality and limitations as a contrast to the old western "universalism" or the mechanics of multiculturalist inclusiveness. It grasps places/latitudes/longitudes without leveling cultural differences.

Curator as Writer

The recent debates on the notion of "Curator as…" speak of a welcome self-reflexivity and plurality of approach. Conventionally, the curator has been expected to be a mediator and an interpreter of art works. However, with increasing numbers of exhibitions that rely heavily on contexts, the curator actually functions as an author. Today, it is easy to see the arrival of "curator as artist/exhibition designer" (Harald Szeemann's term) or "curator as producer" (Hans Ulrich Obrist's term), as a new group of curators, members of the intellectual community attracting artists with diverse cultural backgrounds, begins to form as exhibitions are being opened up into the social sphere. They challenge the traditional boundary of curating by reshaping the exhibition space and recreating the relationship with the viewer. They are eager to suggest new ways of engaging with artworks and they attempt to present the exhibition not as a closed form but as an open space where bureaucratic systems and conventional ideals can be questioned. In a recent essay for *frieze*, Robert Storr said, "I don't think curators are artists. And if they insist, then they will ultimately be judged bad curators as well as bad artists."[7] Such a position turns a blind eye towards the line of flight or conversions that can emerge between the two positions. By getting tied up in the infinite explanation of the interpretation that there is something offensive in the curator's role, such a position ironically ends up reinforcing the idea of curator-as-king, or as forming the majority party within an established order.

Recent changes in the definition of curatorial practices often come across in expressions such as "curator as artist" or "curator as producer." This phenomenon is sometimes considered a manifestation of artist-envy. These criticisms can be used as a defense mechanism of a continual preoccupation of dominant power and its social, psychological, and educational production. The phenomenon of "curator as artist" should not be understood as an attempt to occupy the privileged position of the artist. To me, "curator as artist" comes out of an attempt to invent new devices that can generate different readings of artists and art works. Therefore the relation between curator and artist is not about imitation or mimicry. The question should have nothing to do with the character of this or that exclusive group; it has to do with the transversal relations that ensure that any effects produced in some particular way can always be produced by other means. It is a strange business: each of them finds a real name for themselves, rather, only through the harshest exercise in deper-sonalization, by opening themselves up to the multiplicities everywhere within them, to the intensities running through them. With the curator as artist (such as Harald Szeemann) or the artist as curator (as in Maurizio Cattelan, who was curator of the Berlin Biennale), there are attempts at creating new life and discovering new weapons. It is problematic when an exhibition is reduced to an individual curator, and the works of art within the exhibition take on goals identical to an individual's (thus rendering interpretation important!). This is why Modernist art abounds in manifestos, in ideologies, in theories of art production, at the same time as in personal conflicts, in perfecting of perfections, in neurotic toadying, in narcissistic tribunals. In reality, curating is not an end in itself, precisely because life is not something personal. Rather, the aim of curating is to carry life into the state of a non-personal power. The minimum real unit of an art exhibition is not the work, the idea, the concept or the signifier, but the assemblage. It is always an assemblage that produces time-space images, speeds, lights, and utterances. The assemblage is   co-functioning, "sympathy," symbiosis. Sympathy is different from the claims of the monopoly of being "right." It is not a vague feeling of respect but the exertion of bodies' love or hatred toward each other. The author is first of all a spirit. But the writer is a body operating with a total nervous system. Here we can distinguish two types of curators. The curator as author is a subject of an exhibition (or work) but the curator as writer—someone who is not an author and/or liberated from the politics of the author system—is not the subject. Harald Szeemann, as the pioneer of inventing the notion of "master-narrative" in exhibition making, has been admired as well as criticized. I consider him as an exemplary figure of the curator as writer, because he was a real man of war in making all the elements of a non-homogeneous set converge. The multiple is not only what has many parts, but what folds in many ways. He was original in the way he could make one multiplicity pass into another.

Co-curator System

Biennales today attempt to create containers for cultural translation and meeting points, while emphasizing their locality. Here, subject and object lose their stable status. Hierarchies of the west and non-west disappear, at least on the surface. Subject and object begin to reveal themselves in relation to others, their conflicts and contradictions. After the ideologies of modernity (local vs. global, west vs. non-west and center vs. margin) began to be challenged, the need for solving the problems of unequal cultural exchanges and cultural translations has become an urgent matter; in the age of culture on the border, collaboration becomes inevitable. Paralleling collaboration exercised by the CEO of multi-national corporations, curators have begun to argue for plural authorship, declaring the value of negotiation and the social intervention of art. After Manifesta 1's invention of the co-curator system (1996) and the 2nd Gwangju Biennale's adoption of the system (even Harald Szeemann accepted the suggestion of the co-curator system in 1997), it is no longer universal to concentrate complete and total power upon one authoritative curator. James Clifford argues, "the very idea of plural authorship challenges a deep western identification of any text's order with the intention of a single author."[8] In art, plural authorship, which heavily depends on "post-" discourse, contributed to the advent of "global art" and solidarity among a certain group of curators. However, it is important to note that the co-curator system should not be understood as plural as opposed to singular. Despite the fact that the co-curator system is practically necessary, it should not be confused with the notion of multiplicity in exhibition making. Multiplicity is not determined by the number of curators, artists or works of art. Multiplicity does not mean collection of individual components. It indicates something that is occurring at interstice. For instance, the Lyon Biennale by the Dijon Consortium in 2003 was very successful as an embodiment of the notion of multiplicity. It inspired the viewer to be able to experience interstice phenomenologically. Most biennales are not successful in realizing multiplicity. In the information era, we often attempt to repaint art and its audience with the colors of opinions and communication. Borrowing from Deleuze, it is a spirit of creation that we are lacking, not of communication. Therefore, the number of curators in exhibition making does not have to be a primary concern. A single curator can make a multiplicity and move into another one without depending on curatorial friendship.

Homogenization of the Biennale

Curators are often blamed and asked to take responsibility for the homogenization of Biennales. It is true that curators have contributed to this phenomenon to a certain degree but it is more important to understand the structural causes that lead to homogenization. Most host cities attempt to be part of the transnational global culture through biennales and these efforts often result in blurring the differences among different cultures and contexts. Revealing cultural differences, as opposed to contributing to national or collective identities, which have authentic tradition or history, contradicts the ideology of the nation state and the nature of bureaucracy. International curators who are invited for biennales do not have immediate power to resolve the gap and struggles between the binary poles. The formation of biennales depends on whom the curator gets to work with in the host city or what kind of partnership becomes available. In fact, international biennales in Asian countries are understood as part of the cultural industries by politicians, city officials, local people, and even by local artists; they are not interested in transnational, global contexts or in the issues of contemporary art. Those issues are for a few specialists. The slogan of viewer participation and education appears to have changed the format of biennales, however, it is local politics and their expectations, experience and ethical judgments that influence the contents, direction, and success of a biennale. They expect the biennale to contribute to the publicity of their city and local artists in a short period of time despite the fact that the local contemporary art system is extremely weak. Biennale curators are the ones who understand these expectations best and are meant to be an agent of "global art" anywhere, while providing what they are asked for. They adequately deliver what is expected while creating new cultural issues and networking among major art institutions, emphasizing viewer participation and relations with the local community. In doing so, they construct a new international art language. Biennale exhibitions constantly reproduce certain notions such as hybridity, displacement, difference, marginality, other, representation. It is hard to deny the fact that the group of biennale curators has been successful in attacking modernist viewpoints based on historicism, universal aesthetics, and the hierarchy of an existing system. Their criticism and activities have also generated confusion and conflict and affected non-western art scenes where the division between the west and non-west, between the original and the copy and between the center and the margin was stable. Their activities have gradually been embraced by major art institutions around the world and they are considered as apostles of "global art"; their solidarity signified the symbolic battlefront of global art. Whether it is voluntarily created or not, the co-curator system, however, tends to strengthen the inner circle.

Conclusion

> A traitor to the world of dominant significations, and to the established order. ... The trickster claims to conquer a territory, or even to introduce a new order. The trickster has plenty of future, but no becoming whatsoever. The priest, the soothsayer, is a trickster, but the experimenter is a traitor. The statesman or the courtier is a trickster, but the man of war (not a marshal or a general) is a traitor. ... Many people dream of being traitors. They believe in it, they believe that they are. But they are just petty tricksters. ...What trickster has not said to himself: 'Oh, at last I am a real traitor.' But what traitor does not say to himself at the day's end: 'After all, I was nothing but a trickster.' For it is difficult to be a traitor; it is to create. One has to lose one's identity, one's face, in it. One has to disappear, to become unknown.
> —Gilles Deleuze with Claire Parnet[9]

In order to avoid being a trickster, a curator has to break down major languages and apparatuses that always attempt to engulf multiplicity into the system. Then, the curatorial space will become a sympathetic world for those who are willing to walk the path of becoming, not power and not counterpart. Maurizio Cattelan and the curatorial team of the 4th Berlin Biennale created a unique exhibition by making the best out of the characteristics of the venue: the Jewish Girls' school and its vernacular and ruined characteristics. Works of art dissolved into the historical place and created a new landscape. They were presented as marks of death on a human face whose life has reached its limits. Curators transformed the artists into unknown singers so that the author disappears and the works of art become the refrain that is successfully repeated to create a particular song. In fact, all minorities are the ones whose faces are erased. As we walk into them, we enter signs which escape translation. This biennale does not consider culture as knowledge and does not attempt to invent any discourses. I believe that exhibition making can be an exciting and different process by which the world, class, and the majority one belongs to can be betrayed. Curatorial courses often tend to teach how to join the majority and how to acquire the status of a star curator. We teach and learn how to adapt the trickster mechanism.

Cautionary Tales

1. Henri Lefebvre, *The Production of Space* (Oxford: Blackwell Publishing, 1991), p. 483.
2. Gilles Deleuze and Félix Guattari, *A Thousand Plateaus* (London: Continuum International Publishing Group Ltd., 2004), pp. 544-546.
3. Maria Lind, "On the Edge: Art, Architecture, Design," *Lier & Boog - Series of Philosophy of Art and Art Theory*, Volume 16: Exploding Aesthetics.
4. Homi Bhabha, *The Location of Culture* (London: Routledge, 1994), Chapter 8.
5. Gerardo Mosquera, "Alien-Own/Own-Alien: Globalization and Cultural Difference," *Boundary 2*, Volume 29, Number 3, Fall 2002, pp. 163-173.
6. Gilles Deleuze with Félix Guattari, *What is Philosophy* (New York: Columbia University Press, 1996), p. 110.
7. Robert Storr, "Reading Circle," *frieze*, issue 93, September, 2005.
8. James Clifford, The Predicament of Culture: Twentieth-Century Ethnography, Literature, and Art (Cambridge: Harvard University Press, 2002), p. 51.
9. Gilles Deleuze with Claire Parnet, *Dialogues II* (New York: Columbia University Press, 2002), p. 41.

Translated by Jiyoon Moon.

Young Chul Lee is currently associate professor of Kaywon School of Art and Design and the exhibition and program director at Total Museum of Contemporary Art in Seoul, Korea. He was Artistic Director of the 2nd Gwangju Biennale (1997) and has curated a number of exhibitions including the 2nd Busan Biennale (2000), *D.I.Y. Beyond Instruction* at Total Museum, Seoul (2003), *Mr. Moon on the moon*, *Stranger than paradise,* and *You are My Sunshine* at Total Museum (2004), *Wonderful Travel Agency*, Borusan Gallery, Istanbul, Turkey (2004), The 1st Anyang Public Art Project, Anyang, Korea (2005), and The 3rd Echigo-tsmari Art Triennale, Japan (2006). He has written on art and served on a number of visual art juries. In 2001 he received The Curator of the Year award from the World Curator Association and in 2004 The Best Curator Selected by Curators, Art in Culture.

Additional Reading

Alexander, Victoria D. *Sociology of the Arts*. Oxford: Blackwell Publishing, 2003.

Arthur C. Danto. *After the End of Art*. Princeton: Princeton University Press, 1998.

Attar, Hamdi el. *Exhibition curating & city promotion in cultural activities under globalization*. Taipei: Museum of Contemporary Art Taipei, 2005.

Bauer, Ute Meta. *A new spirit in curating?* Stuttgart: Kunstlerhaus, 1992.

Benjamin Buchloch, "Global Tendencies: Globalism and the Large-Scale Exhibition," a discussion with Francesco Bonami, Catherine David, Okwui Enwezor, Hans-Ulrich Obrist, Martha Rosler, and Yinka Shonibare, mod. James Meyer, intro. Tim Griffin, *Artforum* 52, no. 3 (November 2003): 155.

Berube, Michael, ed. *The Aesthetics of Cultural Studies*. Oxford: Blackwell Publishing, 2004.

Brenson, Michael. "The Curator's Moment" Art journal. 57, no. 4 (1998): 16-27.

Buchloh, B H D and Jean Hubert Martin. "The whole earth show." *Art in America*. New York 77 (5), May 1989: 150-159, 211-213.

Byvanck, Valentijn, ed. *Conventions in Contemporary Art: Lectures and Debates*. Rotterdam: Witte de With Center for Contemporary Art, 2002.

Carbonell, Bettina Messias, ed. *Museum Studies*. Oxford: Blackwell Publishing, 2003.

Carrier, David. *Danto and his critics: art history, historiography and After the end of art*. Middletown, CT: Wesleyan University, 1998.

Carrier, David. *Principles of art history writing*. University Park, PA.: Pennsylvania State University Press, 1991.

Carrier, David. *Writing about visual art*. New York: Allworth Press, 2003.

Charlesworth, J. J. "Curating Doubt - Curators are caught between a rock of narcissism and a hard place of critical paralysis." *Art monthly*. no. 294 (2006): 101-8.

Cooke, Lynne, ed., *Robert Lehman Lectures on Contemporary Art No. 3*. New York: DIA Art Foundation, 2004.

Cream: Contemporary Art in Culture. London: Phaidon, 1998.

Crimp, Douglass. *On the Museum's Ruins*. Cambridge: MIT Press, 1989.

"Curatorial Practice for the 90s" Flash art. no. 191 (1996): 50-3.

Danto, Arthur Coleman. *The wake of art: essays: criticism, philosophy and the ends of taste*. Australia: G+B Arts Int'l, 1998

Drabble, Barnaby, Dorothee Richter and Eva Schmidt, eds. *Curating Degree Zero: An International Curating Symposium*. Nurnberg: Verlag Moderne Kunst Nurnberg, 1999.

Fahy, Anne. *Collections Management*. London; New York: Routledge, 1995.

Fisher, Jean, ed. *Global visions: towards a new internationalism in the visual arts*. London: Kala Press in association with the Institute of International Visual Arts, 1994.

Fowle, Kate and Deborah Smith, eds. *To be continued: contemporary art in practice in public places*. London: Batsford, 2002.

Greenberg, Reesa, Bruce Ferguson and Sandy Nairne, eds. *Thinking about Exhibitions*. New York: Routledge, 1996.

Greenberg, Reesa. "Identity exhibitions: from Magiciens de la terre to Documenta 11." *Art Journal*, Spring, 2005.

Groys, Boris. *Artforum* December 1999.

Groys, Boris. *The Art Judgment Show*. ed. Barbara Vanderlinden Brussels: Roomade, 2001.

Harding, Anna, ed. *Curating the Contemporary Art Museum and Beyond*. London: Academy Editions, 1997 (Art + Design Series, no. 52).

Hawthorne, Christopher, Mark Schapiro and Andras Szanto, eds. *The new gate keepers: emerging challenges to free expression in the arts*. New York: National Arts Journalism Program, Columbia University, 2003.

Hickey, Dave. "On beauty - Buying the world" *Daedalus: proceedings of the American Academy of Arts and Sciences*. 131, no. 4 (2002): 69-88.

Hickey, Dave. *Air guitar: essays on art & democracy*. Los Angeles: Art issues Press; New York: Distributed by D.A.P. (Distributed Art Publishers), 1997.

Hickey, Dave. *The Invisible Dragon: Four Essays on Beauty*. Los Angeles: Art issues Press, 1993.

Hiller, Susan and Sarah Martin, eds. *The producers: contemporary curators in conversation*. 5. Gateshead: BALTIC, 2002.

Hirsh, Mary Rose. *Distrusting art: the conflicted mission of curatorial practice*. Dissertation: Thesis (M.A.)--School of the Art Institute of Chicago, 2004.

Hlavajova, Maria and Jill Winder, eds. *Who if not we should at least try to imagine the future of all this?* Amsterdam: Artimo, 2004.

Hoffmann, Jens and Gioni, Massimiliano. "New Voices in Curating" *Flash art*, no. 222 (2002): 57-61.

Hoffmann, Jens. "New Voices in Curating Part Two" *Flash art*, no. 228 (2003): 57-61.

Hooper-Greenhill, Eilean. *Museums and the Shaping of Knowledge*. London; New York: Routledge, 1992.

Hughes, Lindsay. "Do we need new spaces for exhibiting contemporary art? A critique of cura-torial practice in relation to the viewer's engagement with contemporary art" *Journal of Visual Art Practice* 4, no. 1 (2005): 29-38.

Hutchinson, M. "Curating" *Art monthly*. no. 277, (2004): 44.

Huttner, Per ed. *Curatorial Mutiny*. Stockholm: Farringer Curatorial Mutiny, 2002.

Jacob, Mary Jane, ed. *Culture in Action*. Seattle: Bay Press, 1995.

Kaptein, Helen. *The changing role of the museum curator*. Thesis (M. Museum Studies)--Deakin University, Victoria, 1997.

Kapur, Geeta. "Globalisation and culture." *Third text: Third World perspectives on contempo-rary art & culture*. London No. 39, summer 1997: 21-38.

Kapur, Geeta. *When was modernism: essays on contemporary cultural practice in India*. New Delhi: Tulika, 2000.

Kocar, Zoya and Simon Leung, eds. *Theory in Contemporary Art since 1985*. Oxford: Blackwell Publishing, 2004.

Kortun, Vasif and Hanru Hou. *How latitudes become forms: art in a global age*. Minneapolis: Walker Art Center, 2003.

Krysa, Joasia, ed. *Curating Immateriality: The Work of the Curator in the Age of Network Systems*. Brooklyn, NY: Autonomedia, 2006.

Kuoni, Carin, ed. *Words of Wisdom: A Curator's Vade Mecum on Contemporary Art*. New York: Independent Curators International, 2001.

Macdonald, Sharon, ed. *A Companion to Museum Studies*. Oxford: Blackwell Publishing, 2006.

Marcus, George E. and Fred R. Myers, eds., *The Traffic in Culture: Refiguring Art and Anthropology*. Berkeley: University of California Press, 1995.

Marincola, Paula, ed. *Curating Now: Imaginative Practice/Public Responsibility*. Philadelphia: Philadelphia Exhibitions Initiative, 2001.

Marstine, Janet, ed. *New Museum Theory and Practice*. Oxford: Blackwell Publishing, 2006.

Martin, Jean-Hubert ; Zolghadr, Tirdad "Debate: Ethnocentrism" *Frieze: contemporary art and culture*, no. 88 (2005): 72-3.

Martin, Jean-Hubert. "Art in a multi-ethnic society." *Africus*: Johannesburg Biennale, 20 February-30 April, 1995.

Napack, Jonathan. "Alternative visions: in a provocative curatorial gesture, this year's Gwangju Biennale was largely dedicated to-and determined by-independent artist groups and alternative spaces - Report From Gwangju - Critical Essay." *Art in America*, 90, no. 11, November 2002: 94-122.

Newman, Michael and Jon Bird, eds. *Rewriting Conceptual Art*. London: Reaktion Books, 1999.

Noever, Peter, ed. *The Discursive Museum*. Ostfildern: Hatje Cantz, 2001.

O'Neill, P. "Curating Degree Zero Archive" *Art monthly*. no. 288, (2005): 40-41.

Obrist, Hans Ulrich, Rehberg, Vivian and Boeri, Stefano. "Moving Interventions: Curating at Large" *Journal of Visual Culture* 2, no. 2 (2003): 147-160.

Phaidon Press, eds. *Fresh Cream*. London: Phaidon, 2000.

Pick, John and Malcolm Hey Anderton. *Arts Administration*. London; New York: E & FN Spon, 1996.

Putnam, James. *Art and Artifact: The Museum as Medium*. New York: Thames and Hudson, 2001.

Rectanus, Mark W. *Culture Incorporated: Museums, Artists, and Corporate Sponsorships*. Minneapolis: University of Minnesota Press, 2002.

Rugoff, Ralph. "Rules of the Game," *frieze*, vol. 44 (Jan-Feb 1999): 46-49.

Rugoff, Ralph. *You talking to me?: On curating group shows that give you a chance to join the group*. Philadelphia: Philadelphia Exhibitions Initiative, 2003.

Schubert, Karsten. *The Curator's Egg: the evolution of the museum concept from the French Revolution to the present day*. London: One-Off Press, 2000.

Selz, Peter Howard and Kristine Stiles, eds. *Theories and Documents of Contemporary Art: A Sourcebook of Artists' Writings*. Berkeley: University of California Press, 1996.

Smiers, Joost. *Arts Under Pressure: Promoting Cultural Diversity in the Age of Globalization*. London & NY: Zed Books Ltd., 2003.

Smith, Paul and Carolyn Wilde, eds. *A Companion to Art Theory*. Oxford; Malden, MA: Blackwell Publishing, 2002.

Strauss, David Levi. *Between dog & wolf: essays on art and politics in the twilight of the millennium*. New York: Autonomedia, 1999.

Strauss, David Levi. *Between the eyes: essays on photography and politics*. New York: Aperture, 2003.

Sullivan, Graeme. *Art Practice As Research: Inquiry in the Visual Arts*. Thousand Oaks, CA: Sage Publications Inc, 2005.

The Manual of New Curatorship looks set to define curatorial roles in the 1990s. *Museums journal*. 92, no. 10 (October 1992): 50.

The Next Documenta Should Be Curated By An Artist Frankfurt: REVOLVER-Archiv fur aktuelle Kunst, 2004.

Thea, Carolee, ed. *Foci: Interivews with Ten International Curators*. New York: apexart, 2001.

Thomas, Catherine, ed. *The Edge of Everything: Reflections on Curatorial Practice*, Banff: Banff Centre Press, 2002.

Timms, Peter. *What's Wrong With Contemporary Art?* Sydney: University of New South Wales Press, 2004.

Townsend, Melanie, ed. *Beyond the Box: Diverging Curatorial Practices*, Banff: Banff Centre Press, 2003.

Wade, Gavin, ed. *Curating in the 21st Century*. Walsall, England: Walsall Local History Centre, 2001.

Weil, Stephen E. *Making Museums Matter*. Washington D.C.: Smithsonian Institution Press, 2002.

White, Peter, ed. *Naming a Practice: Curatorial Strategies for the Future*. Banff: Banff Centre Press, 1996.

Witcomb, Andrea. *Re-Imagining the Museum: Beyond the Mausoleum*. London; New York: Routledge, 2003.

Wu, Chin-tao. *Privatising Culture: Corporate Art Intervention Since the 1980s*. London and NY: Verso, 2002.

Cover Image Credits

Front cover, top row, left to right:

Magiciens de la Terre installation image courtesy Jean-Hubert Martin; Photo: Jaeques Faujour

Installation view of *Beau Monde: Toward a Redeemed Cosmopolitanism* curated by Dave Hickey. Foreground (reflected in mirror): Jessica Stockholder, *Bird Watching*, 2001; Darryl Montana, *Judy's Garden*, 2000. Background (through doorway): Pia Fries, *quinto*, 1994-1995; James Lee Byars, *Eros*, 1992; Bridget Riley, *Evoe I*, 1999-2000; Photo: Herbert Lotz

documenta1 installation image © documenta Archiv Photographer: Gunther Becker

Utopia Station exhibition installation image courtesy Hans Ulrich Obrist

Front cover, bottom row, left to right:

The Art of 9/11 installation of exhibition curated by Arthur Danto at apexart 2005

When Attitudes Become Form (1969) exhibition installation image courtesy Kunsthalle Bern

From *Bombay/Mumbai 1992-2001* co-curated by Geeta Kapur and Ashish Rajadhyaksha for the exhibition *Century City: Art and Culture in the Modern Metropolis*, Tate Modern, 2001. View in the Turbine Hall: Sen Kapadia, *Pandal* (2001, cloth and bamboo site-specific cinema hall mounted with a hand-painted Bollywood film poster); foreground, Kausik Mukhopadhyay, *15-part, Assisted Ready-Mades: Chairs* (2000, mixed media). Photo: Anthony Stokes

Cities on the Move exhibition installation image courtesy Hans Ulrich Obrist

Back cover, left to right, top row:

When Attitudes Become Form (1969) exhibition installation image courtesy Kunsthalle Bern

Something Happened installation of exhibition curated by Sally Berger at apexart 2000

2003 Summer Program installation of exhibition curated by Katy Siegel at apexart 2003

A view of the south wall in Room 3, in *Enartete Kunst*, Munich 1937, *"Degenerate Art" the fate of the Avant-Guarde in Nazi Germany*, 1991; Photograph courtesy of Museum Associates/LACMA

Back cover, left to right, bottom row:

Magiciens de la Terre installation image courtesy Jean-Hubert Martin; Photo: Jaeques Faujour

Mixology installation of exhibition curated by Dave Hickey at apexart 1999

Between the Lines installation of exhibition curated by Rebecca Gordon Nesbitt at apexart 2003

From *Bombay/Mumbai 1992-2001* co-curated by Geeta Kapur and Ashish Rajadhyaksha for the exhibition *Century City: Art and Culture in the Modern Metropolis*, Tate Modern, 2001. View in the Turbine Hall: Vivan Sundaram, *Gun Carriage from the installation Memorial* (1993-2000, photograph, acrylic sheet, iron, glass, steel). Far wall: detail of Atul Dodiya, *Missing*, detail (2000, enamel paint on metal roller shutters and laminate boards); Photo: Anthony Stokes